Deporting Immigrants

Other Books in the Current Controversies Series

Deporting Immigrants

Anne Cunningham, Book Editor

GREENHAVEN
PUBLISHING

Published in 2018 by Greenhaven Publishing, LLC
353 3rd Avenue, Suite 255, New York, NY 10010

Articles in Greenhaven Publishing anthologies are often edited for length to meet page
requirements. In addition, original titles of these works are changed to clearly present
the main thesis and to explicitly indicate the author's opinion. Every effort is made to
ensure that Greenhaven Publishing accurately reflects the original intent of the authors.
Every effort has been made to trace the owners of the copyrighted material.

Cover image: Drew Angerer/Getty Images

Library of Congress Cataloging-in-Publication Data

Names: Cunningham, Anne C., editor.
Title: Deporting immigrants / Anne Cunningham, book editor.
Description: First edition. | New York : Greenhaven Publishing, [2018] |
   Series: Current controversies | Includes bibliographical references and
   index. | Audience: Grade 9 to 12.
Identifiers: LCCN 2017041743| ISBN 9781534502345 (library bound) | ISBN
   9781534502406 (pbk.)
Subjects: LCSH: Illegal aliens--Government policy--United States--Juvenile
   literature. | Deportation--United States--Juvenile literature. | United
   States--Emigration and immigration--Government policy--Juvenile literature.
Classification: LCC JV6483 .D46 2017 | DDC 325.73--dc23
LC record available at https://lccn.loc.gov/2017041743

Manufactured in the United States of America

Website: http://greenhavenpublishing.com

Contents

Chapter 1: Does US Immigration Policy Have Its Roots in Racism?

> *Muzaffar Chishti, Faye Hipsman, and Isabel Ball*
> The 1965 Immigration and Nationality Act ushered in the modern era of US immigration policy. Its lasting achievement was to finally repeal discriminatory quotas based on country of origin.

Yes: Racism Is the Foundation of US Immigration Policy

> *Doug Chin*
> Chinese immigrants provided much of the labor required for US westward expansion. When jobs became scarce, the Chinese Exclusion Act was passed to protect white workers from competition.

> *Adrian Florido*
> Trump's campaign promise to deport 11 million immigrants is nothing new. In the 1930s, millions of Mexicans and Americans of Mexican descent were repatriated en masse.

No: Early US Immigration Laws Reflect a Complex History

> *Ted Gong*
> The 2011–2012 Congress passed H. Res. 683 and H. Res. 282 condemning the Chinese Exclusion Act of 1882. Constituents overwhelmingly supported formal censure of this blight on the nation's history.

Chapter 2: Have Deportation and Immigration Policies Gotten Worse in the New Millennium?

Yes: The Obama Administration Aggressively Pursued Deportations

Chapter 3: Can Deportation in the Age of Trump Be a Boon to America?

Yes: Trump's Executive Actions on Immigration Are Defensible Policy

Jacqueline Varas

The stated purpose of Trump's action on immigration is to protect public safety in the US interior, secure the nation's borders, and prevent those who wish to harm citizens from entering the country.

Salim Mansur

Trump's temporary immigration ban on seven Muslim majority countries was met with widespread condemnation. Here, a writer argues that the restriction is necessary, as it will force the Muslim world to address instability and violence.

No: Travel Bans and Mass Deportations Are the Wrong Move

Alice Miranda Ollstein

According to multiple reports, travelers from the Muslim majority countries targeted by Trump's controversial immigration ban were pressured by CBP agents to sign away their rights.

Teresa Wiltz

President Trump pledged to focus deportation efforts on serious criminals, much like his predecessor. The rate of violent crime among undocumented immigrants is lower than that of US citizens, and many are being removed for minor offenses.

Foreword

"Controversy" is a word that has an undeniably unpleasant connotation. It carries a definite negative charge. Controversy can spoil family gatherings, spread a chill around classroom and campus discussion, inflame public discourse, open raw civic wounds, and lead to the ouster of public officials. We often feel that controversy is almost akin to bad manners, a rude and shocking eruption of that which must not be spoken or thought of in polite, tightly guarded society. To avoid controversy, to quell controversy, is often seen as a public good, a victory for etiquette, perhaps even a moral or ethical imperative.

Yet the studious, deliberate avoidance of controversy is also a whitewashing, a denial, a death threat to democracy. It is a false sterilizing and sanitizing and superficial ordering of the messy, ragged, chaotic, at times ugly processes by which a healthy democracy identifies and confronts challenges, engages in passionate debate about appropriate approaches and solutions, and arrives at something like a consensus and a broadly accepted and supported way forward. Controversy is the megaphone, the speaker's corner, the public square through which the citizenry finds and uses its voice. Controversy is the life's blood of our democracy and absolutely essential to the vibrant health of our society.

Our present age is certainly no stranger to controversy. We are consumed by fierce debates about technology, privacy, political correctness, poverty, violence, crime and policing, guns, immigration, civil and human rights, terrorism, militarism, environmental protection, and gender and racial equality. Loudly competing voices are raised every day, shouting opposing opinions, putting forth competing agendas, and summoning starkly different visions of a utopian or dystopian future. Often these voices attempt to shout the others down; there is precious little listening and considering among the cacophonous din. Yet listening and considering, too, are essential to the health of a democracy. If controversy is democracy's lusty lifeblood, respectful listening and careful thought are its higher faculties, its brain, its conscience.

Current Controversies does not shy away from or attempt to hush the loudly competing voices. It seeks to provide readers with as wide and representative as possible a range of articulate voices on any given controversy of the day, separates each one out to allow it to be heard clearly and fairly, and encourages careful listening to each of these well-crafted, thoughtfully expressed opinions, supplied by some of today's leading academics, thinkers, analysts, politicians, policy makers, economists, activists, change agents, and advocates. Only after listening to a wide range of opinions on an issue, evaluating the strengths and weaknesses of each argument, assessing how well the facts and available evidence mesh with the stated opinions and conclusions, and thoughtfully and critically examining one's own beliefs and conscience can the reader begin to arrive at his or her own conclusions and articulate his or her own stance on the spotlighted controversy.

This process is facilitated and supported in each Current Controversies volume by an introduction and chapter overviews that provide readers with the essential context they need to begin engaging with the spotlighted controversies, with the debates surrounding them, and with their own perhaps shifting or nascent opinions on them. Chapters are organized around several key questions that are answered with diverse opinions representing all points on the political spectrum. In its content, organization, and methodology, readers are encouraged to determine the authors' point of view and purpose, interrogate and analyze the various arguments and their rhetoric and structure, evaluate the arguments' strengths and weaknesses, test their claims against available facts and evidence, judge the validity of the reasoning, and bring into clearer, sharper focus the reader's own beliefs and conclusions and how they may differ from or align with those in the collection or those of classmates.

Research has shown that reading comprehension skills improve dramatically when students are provided with compelling, intriguing, and relevant "discussable" texts. The subject matter of these collections could not be more compelling, intriguing, or urgently relevant to today's students and the world they are poised to inherit. The anthologized articles also provide the basis for stimulating, lively, and passionate classroom debates. Students who are compelled to anticipate objections to their own argument and identify the flaws in those of an opponent read more carefully, think more critically, and steep themselves in relevant context, facts, and information more thoroughly. In short, using discussable text of the kind provided by every single volume in the Current Controversies series encourages close reading, facilitates reading comprehension, fosters research, strengthens critical thinking, and greatly enlivens and energizes classroom discussion and participation. The entire learning process is deepened, extended, and strengthened.

If we are to foster a knowledgeable, responsible, active, and engaged citizenry, we must provide readers with the intellectual, interpretive, and critical-thinking tools and experience necessary to make sense of the world around them and of the all-important debates and arguments that inform it. We must encourage them not to run away from or attempt to quell controversy but to embrace it in a responsible, conscientious, and thoughtful way, to sharpen and strengthen their own informed opinions by listening to and critically analyzing those of others. This series encourages respectful engagement with and analysis of current controversies and competing opinions and fosters a resulting increase in the strength and rigor of one's own opinions and stances. As such, it helps readers assume their rightful place in the public square and provides them with the skills necessary to uphold their awesome responsibility—guaranteeing the continued and future health of a vital, vibrant, and free democracy.

Introduction

We have all heard the phrase "the United States is a nation of immigrants" countless times. In truth, immigration is a far more complex issue than this cliché would suggest. True, the United States has welcomed countless from around the globe, but America has never endorsed an open door policy for the so-called huddled masses. Preferential treatment for some groups, and brutal discrimination against others, yields a history marked as much by injustice, racism, and violence as by the embrace of newcomers.

For those lacking the criteria for legal immigration, such as a family relationship to a US citizen, financial resources, or employment skills, documented entry to the United States is not always a viable option. Many immigrants undertake a perilous journey to escape economic hardship or danger. Sadly, a jarring process known as deportation is likely to await the undocumented at their destination. Despite this heartbreaking fact, most agree that the United States cannot absorb everyone who wishes to enter. Indeed, in the past few decades, US authorities have deported millions of undocumented immigrants. Is this fair? Can the system be reformed to be more humane and egalitarian?

"Deportation" is a broad term subsuming the more specific processes of apprehension, removal, and return. One immigrant may be turned away at the border for administrative reasons, while another might voluntarily return to his or her country of origin. Both are said to be deportees, though the latter may self-deport due to threats and intimidation arising outside the legitimate structure of federal immigration law. In the 1930s, for example, up to two million Mexicans and Mexican Americans were deported in a manner euphemistically referred to as "repatriation." In this shameful, rarely studied episode of American history, an estimated 60 percent of deportees were actually American citizens of Mexican decent.

Historically, heavy waves of immigration have been accompanied by xenophobic sentiment. Immigrants are routinely made scapegoats for native economic anxiety, regardless of their role in the labor market. Ethnic and national groups deemed unwanted by the social and political realities of the day, typically the most recent arrivals on US shores, are generally the most vulnerable to harassment and deportation. This is especially true during economic downturns, as the era of Chinese exclusion, the Great Depression, and our current moment all illustrate.

In the nineteenth century, Chinese immigrant labor was instrumental to the growth of the western US economy, particularly the mining and railroad industries. Nonetheless, the Chinese Exclusion Act of 1882 openly discriminated against this group. The law prevented Chinese laborers from competing against whites for increasingly scarce jobs and included poll taxes and restrictions on Chinese testimony against whites in court. Emboldened by this law, violence and arson were used to intimidate Chinese. The most lasting legacy of the Chinese Exclusion Act was to establish a quota system. This remained the law of the land for almost a century.

In 1965, the Hart-Celler Act repealed national-origins quotas designed to favor immigration from Europe. It is not surprising that "white" nations were favored, as quotas were proposed at a time when theories of eugenics circulated widely. The 1965 law created a preference system based on immigrants' family relationships with US citizens or legal permanent residents and, to a lesser degree, their skills. The above criteria remained the cornerstone of immigration policy for decades.

Securing US borders became a political priority after the terrorist attacks of 2001. In 2003, under the rubric of the Department of Homeland Security (DHS), Border Protection (CBP) and Immigration and Customs Enforcement (ICE) both nearly doubled in size. In addition, over 70 measures instilling cooperation and coordination between local and federal authorities went into effect. More powerful data enabled efficient enforcement. As a result, removals increased massively throughout the 2000s.

President Obama inherited this situation but has been criticized for ramping up deportations. Defenders claim his policies target only serious criminals and allow the law abiding and their children to pursue paths to citizenship. There is evidence Obama's immigration enforcement strategies have been less sanguine than defenders claim: only half received hearings, and about a third had children or spouses who are US citizens. Moreover, many deportees were removed for minor infractions such as traffic tickets. The epithet "deporter in chief" hung over Obama's presidency, but his administration rarely, if ever, deployed hostile rhetoric against immigrants. The same cannot be said of his successor.

The 2016 presidential election brought deportation back to the national conversation. On the campaign trail, Donald Trump made multiple racist remarks against Mexicans too crude to repeat, and he promised to deport "bad hombres" and to build a border wall at Mexico's expense. Blaming immigrants for economic frustration was hardly an original or honorable tactic, but it tapped into deep resentments and helped get him elected. It remains to be seen whether a border wall will materialize or if Trump's deportation record will break significantly with previous US presidents of the twenty-first century. If the first six months are any indication, ICE raids and other tactics of fear and intimidation will not bode well for immigrant communities.

The viewpoints this reader comprises cover issues pertaining to deportation, from the nineteenth century to the present. An examination of this history reveals recurring patterns—some cruel, others hopeful. To jettison our worst impulses and foster meaningful reform for social progress, familiarity with this narrative is absolutely essential. What follows is an effort to present key information on immigration and deportation in a coherent, organized, and readable fashion.

Does US Immigration Policy Have Its Roots in Racism?

Overview: The Enduring Legacy of the 1965 Immigration and Nationality Act

Muzaffar Chishti, Faye Hipsman, and Isabel Ball

Muzaffar Chishti, Faye Hipsman, and Isabel Ball contribute to Policy Beat for the Migration Policy Institute.

October 2015 marks the 50th anniversary of the seminal Immigration and Nationality Act of 1965. Signed into law at the foot of the Statue of Liberty by President Lyndon B. Johnson, the act ushered in far-reaching changes that continue to undergird the current immigration system, and set in motion powerful demographic forces that are still shaping the United States today and will in the decades ahead.

The law, known as the Hart-Celler Act for its congressional sponsors, literally changed the face of America. It ended an immigration-admissions policy based on race and ethnicity, and gave rise to large-scale immigration, both legal and unauthorized. While the anniversary has provided an opportunity to reflect on the law's historic significance, it also reminds us that the '65 Act holds important lessons for policymaking today.

The Significance of the 1965 Act, Then and Now

The historic significance of the 1965 law was to repeal national-origins quotas, in place since the 1920s, which had ensured that immigration to the United States was primarily reserved for European immigrants. The 1921 national-origins quota law was enacted in a special congressional session after President Wilson's pocket veto. Along with earlier and other contemporary statutory bars to immigration from Asian countries, the quotas

"Fifty Years On, the 1965 Immigration and Nationality Act Continues to Reshape the United States" by Muzaffar Chishti, Faye Hipsman, and Isabel Ball, Migration Information Source (the online journal of the Migration Policy Institute), October 15, 2015, http://www.migrationpolicy.org/article/fifty-years-1965-immigration-and-nationality-act-continues-reshape-united-states. Reprinted by permission.

were proposed at a time when eugenics theories were widely accepted. The quota for each country was set at 2 percent of the foreign-born population of that nationality as enumerated in the 1890 census. The formula was designed to favor Western and Northern European countries and drastically limit admission of immigrants from Asia, Africa, the Middle East, and Southern and Eastern Europe. In major revisions to U.S. immigration law in 1952, the national-origins system was retained, despite a strong veto message by President Truman.

Building on a campaign promise by President Kennedy, and with a strong push by President Johnson amid the enactment of other major civil-rights legislation, the 1965 law abolished the national-origins quota system. It was replaced with a preference system based on immigrants' family relationships with U.S. citizens or legal permanent residents and, to a lesser degree, their skills. The law placed an annual cap of 170,000 visas for immigrants from the Eastern Hemisphere, with no single country allowed more than 20,000 visas, and for the first time established a cap of 120,000 visas for immigrants from the Western Hemisphere. Three-fourths of admissions were reserved for those arriving in family categories. Immediate relatives (spouses, minor children, and parents of adult U.S. citizens) were exempt from the caps; 24 percent of family visas were assigned to siblings of U.S. citizens. In 1976, the 20,000 per country limit was applied to the Western Hemisphere. And in 1978, a worldwide immigrant visa quota was set at 290,000.

Though ratified half a century ago, the Hart-Celler framework still defines today's legal immigration system. Under current policy, there are five family-based admissions categories, ranked in preference based on the family relationship, and capped at 480,000 visas (again, exempting immediate relatives of U.S. citizens), and five employment-based categories capped at 140,000 visas. Smaller numbers are admitted through refugee protection channels and the Diversity Visa Lottery—a program designed to bring immigrants from countries that are underrepresented in U.S.

immigration streams, partly as a consequence of the 1965 Act. Though Congress passed the Immigration Act of 1990 to admit a greater share of highly skilled and educated immigrants through employment channels, family-based immigrants continue to comprise two-thirds of legal immigration, while about 15 percent of immigrants become permanent residents through their employers.

Unintended Consequences

Much of the sweeping impact of the 1965 Immigration and Nationality Act was the result of unintended consequences. "The bill that we sign today is not a revolutionary bill," President Johnson said during the signing ceremony. "It does not affect the lives of millions. It will not reshape the structure of our daily lives, or really add importantly to either our wealth or our power." Senator Ted Kennedy (D-MA), the bill's floor manager, stated: "It will not upset the ethnic mix of our society." Even advocacy groups who had favored the national-origins quotas became supporters, predicting little change to the profile of immigration streams.

Despite these predictions, the measure had a profound effect on the flow of immigrants to the United States, and in only a matter of years began to transform the U.S. demographic profile. The number of new lawful permanent residents (or green-card holders) rose from 297,000 in 1965 to an average of about 1 million each year since the mid-2000s. Accordingly, the foreign-born population has risen from 9.6 million in 1965 to a record high of 45 million in 2015 as estimated by a new study from the Pew Research Center Hispanic Trends Project. Immigrants accounted for just 5 percent of the U.S. population in 1965 and now comprise 14 percent.

A second unintended consequence of the law stemmed largely from a political compromise clearly intended to have the opposite effect. The original bill provided a preference for immigrants with needed skills and education. But a group of influential congressmen (conservatives allied with the Democratic chairman of the House immigration subcommittee) won a last-minute concession to prioritize admission of immigrants with family members already in the United States, believing it would better preserve the country's predominantly Anglo-Saxon, European base. In the following years, however, demand from Europeans to immigrate to the United States fell flat while interest from non-European countries—many emerging from the end of colonial rule—began to grow. New and well-educated immigrants from diverse countries in Asia and Latin America established themselves in the United States and became the foothold for subsequent immigration by their family networks.

Compared to almost entirely European immigration under the national-origins system, flows since 1965 have been more than half Latin American and one-quarter Asian. The largest share of today's immigrant population, about 11.6 million, is from Mexico. Together with India, the Philippines, China, Vietnam, El Salvador, Cuba, South Korea, the Dominican Republic, and Guatemala, these ten countries account for nearly 60 percent of the current immigrant population.

In turn, the law dramatically altered the racial and ethnic makeup of the United States. In 1965, whites of European descent comprised 84 percent of the U.S. population, while Hispanics accounted for 4 percent and Asians for less than 1 percent. Fifty years on, 62 percent of the U.S. population is white, 18 percent is Hispanic, and 6 percent is Asian. By 2065, just 46 percent of the U.S. population will be white, the Hispanic share will rise to 24 percent, Asians will comprise 14 percent—and the country will be home to 78 million foreign born, according to Pew projections.

The 1965 Act also inadvertently laid the foundation for the steep rise in illegal immigration since the 1970s. In a parallel development whose impact was not recognized at the time, Congress in 1964 terminated the Bracero program, which since 1942 had been used to recruit temporary agricultural workers from Mexico to fill World War II farm-labor shortages in the United States. In total, 4.6 million Mexican guestworkers were admitted, peaking at 445,000 in 1956. When the guestworker program ended, many former Bracero workers continued crossing the border to fill the same jobs, but now illegally. The combination of the end of the

Bracero program and limits on legal immigration from the Western Hemisphere combined to fuel the rise of illegal immigration.

Implications for Today's Debate

Introduced in January 1965 and signed into law on October 3, the Hart-Celler Act took only nine months to enact. Its swift passage through the 89th Congress raises the question of why today's political leaders have failed for more than a decade to pass substantive immigration legislation. First, passage of the law was truly bipartisan, despite Democratic control of the White House, Senate, and House. In the Senate, the bill was approved by a vote of 76 to 18, with support from 52 Democrats and 24 Republicans. The House passed the bill 320 to 70; 202 Democrats and 117 Republicans supported it, while 60 Democrats and ten Republicans voted against it. Not only did the bill win support from the majorities of both parties in the House and Senate, in each more Democrats opposed the bill than Republicans.

Second, lawmakers approved the measure without significant floor debate—deferring to the expertise of the Judiciary committees and their immigration subcommittees to craft the proposal. Lastly, President Johnson focused his attention not on policy details or advancing the White House's immigration agenda, but on the process of moving the bill forward through Congress. In today's hostile political climate, congressional gridlock, and polarized, high-stakes immigration debate, lawmakers could learn from the process that led to the law's swift passage.

The 1965 Act: A Success or Failure?

Opinions differ on whether the 1965 Act helped or harmed the country. The law's proponents see it as a historic success and assert that the estimated 59 million immigrants who have come to the United States since its passage have made the country younger, infused it with diversity and talent, and generated prosperity and economic growth. Critics contend that high admission levels of diverse groups of immigrants have created more competition for low-skilled U.S. workers and shattered the country's cultural homogeneity.

Despite such misgivings, a recent major study by the National Academies of Sciences, Engineering, and Medicine suggests that post-1965 Act immigrants and their children—estimated to comprise one in four people in the United States—are successfully integrating into U.S. society. The study finds that immigrant integration increases over time and successive generations achieve strong progress in key indicators including education, earnings, language proficiency, and occupational distribution. At the same time, immigrants and their descendants as a whole still lag behind the native-born population on these indicators.

How well post-1965 Act immigrants have integrated has varied substantially, depending on their legal status, social class, educational background, and the geographic area where they settle, the study also found. Profiles of diaspora groups (comprised of immigrants and their U.S.-born descendants) from countries that have dominated post-1965 immigration flows show that many have surpassed median U.S. educational attainment levels, household incomes, and workforce participation rates. The Indian diaspora, for example—numbering 3.8 million—is significantly higher educated, more likely to be employed, and has a higher household income compared to the U.S. population as a whole. The Filipino, Bangladeshi, Pakistani, Egyptian, Kenyan, and Nigerian diasporas tell similar stories, while the diasporas of other countries, such as Ghana, Morocco, Ethiopia, and Colombia are generally on par with medians for the U.S. born on most indicators. Further, the educational levels of newly arrived immigrants have been consistently improving since the 1970s, according to the Pew Hispanic Trends study. In 2013, 41 percent of recently arrived immigrants were college graduates compared to 20 percent in 1970. In comparison, 30 percent of the native-born population had college degrees in 2013 vs. 11 percent in 1970.

While the 1965 law has empowered many diverse immigrants and their families to build new and prosperous lives in the

United States, its unintended consequences have clearly hindered integration for others—particularly diaspora groups whose members are more likely to lack legal status. Mexican immigrants and their descendants (an estimated 34.8 million) are far more socioeconomically disadvantaged than other diaspora groups and have below-average educational attainment and household incomes. The Salvadoran and Haitian diasporas have a similar profile.

At heart, the current U.S. immigration debate is an unresolved cultural conversation about the nation's identity. As the congressional policymaking process remains stalled, many of the dynamics established by the 1965 Immigration and Nationality Act—for better or for worse—are likely to persist. Until there are consequential changes to the immigration system, now a half-century old, the 1965 Act will continue to shape the changing face of America.

National Policy Beat in Brief

Border Apprehensions of Unaccompanied Children and Families on the Rise

The U.S. Border Patrol apprehended 9,790 unaccompanied minors and families at the U.S.-Mexico border in August, a 52 percent increase from the same period last year. Of the total apprehended, 4,632 were unaccompanied children, while the remaining 5,158 were parents traveling with young children (officially referred to as "family units"). The monthly totals are the highest since a surge of children and families arrived at the border in summer 2014, resulting in approximately 69,000 unaccompanied child and 68,000 family apprehensions in fiscal year (FY) 2014. The White House called the August increase a "surprising uptick" and a "concern."

Meanwhile, on September 18, the Obama administration appealed an August federal court ruling in *Flores v. Lynch* that ordered the immediate release of families from immigration detention. The ruling found that the Department of Homeland Security (DHS) had breached a long-standing court settlement that requires immigrant children be held only in facilities licensed to care for children and gave authorities until October 23 to comply.

Obama Administration Increases Aid and Admissions for Syrian Refugees

On September 21, the U.S. Agency for International Development (USAID) announced that the United States would donate an additional $419 million in humanitarian and refugee aid to those affected by the four and a half year conflict in Syria. In total, the United States has donated more than $4.5 billion to Syria relief efforts since 2012. Furthermore, the White House increased the number of Syrian refugees to be resettled in the United States from 2,000 in FY 2015 to 10,000 in FY 2016, which began on October 1. The Obama administration also raised the worldwide refugee admissions ceiling from 70,000 in FY 2015 to 85,000 in FY 2016, and has said the quota will be increased to 100,000 in FY 2017. Many observers argue that although the proposed increases are significant compared to last year's admissions, they do not meet the global demand for resettlement of refugees fleeing war in Syria and other countries in the Middle East.

Obama Administration Revises Proposed Changes to Visa Bulletin

On September 25, the State Department and U.S. Citizenship and Immigration Services (USCIS) announced a reversal to the Visa Bulletin changes proposed earlier in the month. The monthly Visa Bulletin provides information on when statutorily limited visas are available to be issued to prospective immigrants based on their individual priority dates (the filing date of their approved immigrant visa petitions). The proposed changes were part of the president's November 2014 executive actions on immigration and would have allowed certain individuals in the immigrant-visa backlog to submit their permanent residence applications before their priority dates. In anticipation of these changes, it is estimated more than 20,000 immigrants had prepared their applications for filing, which would have enabled the primary applicants and derivative family members to obtain employment authorization and travel documents. The government since said the bulletin was "adjusted to better reflect a timeframe justifying immediate action in the application process." In response to the sudden reversal, a group of high-skilled immigrants filed a federal lawsuit in Seattle claiming damages that arose from expenses related to their legal fees or medical exams.

Cuban Arrivals Rise at Texas Ports of Entry

Between October 2014 and June 2015, approximately 18,520 Cubans arrived at ports of entry in South Texas seeking admission into the United States. If the trend held, the Texas border region would have seen an estimated 24,700 Cuban migrants arrive at land ports between Del Rio and Brownsville by the end of FY 2015, representing a 60 percent increase from FY 2014. The influx is presumed to be in response to a recent decision by Cuba and the United States to normalize diplomatic relations for the first time since 1959. The change has raised concerns among Cubans that their special treatment under United States immigration law could be terminated in the normalization process. The special status of Cubans dates back to the Cuban Adjustment Act of 1966, which allows Cubans arriving in the United States via land ports to be admitted and be eligible to apply for lawful permanent residence after one year in the United States. No other country's nationals are afforded similar treatment by U.S. law.

Some Immigrants with Mental Disabilities May Contest Removal under New Court Settlement

American Civil Liberties Union (ACLU) and DHS on September 25 finalized a federal district court settlement allowing eligible immigrants with serious mental illnesses who were ordered deported to reopen their cases with the possibility of returning to the United States. The settlement applies to noncitizens with mental disabilities who were not given a legitimate competency determination and were deported after representing themselves without counsel in immigration court. Under a pair of court orders issued in 2013 and 2014, immigrants with serious mental disabilities facing deportation have a right to legal representation if they are determined not competent to represent themselves, and the government is required to provide such determinations. The settlement applies to noncitizens detained in Arizona, California, and Washington after November 21, 2011. Mental disabilities covered in the settlement include psychosis, bipolar disorder, schizophrenia, and major depressive disorder.

Obama Administration Launches Naturalization Initiative
On September 17, the White House launched a public awareness campaign to encourage eligible legal permanent residents (LPRs) to apply for U.S. citizenship. Of the 13.3 million LPRs in the United States, 8.8 million are eligible to naturalize, according to recent DHS estimates. During the campaign's first week, a variety of businesses and nonprofits hosted more than 70 citizenship outreach events, while the federal government held 200 naturalization ceremonies for more than 36,000 new citizens across the United States. Additionally, USCIS will post online U.S. civics and history practice tests for the naturalization exam that permanent residents are required to pass to become citizens. USCIS will also begin allowing credit card payments of the $680 naturalization fee. The initiative is one component of a series of executive actions on immigration announced by President Obama in November 2014.

State and Local Policy Beat in Brief
North Carolina Legislature Passes E-Verify, Sanctuary Cities, and ID law
On September 29, North Carolina's General Assembly passed the Protect North Carolina Workers Act. The bill prohibits use of identification issued by municipalities, counties, or diplomatic consuls to establish eligibility for state benefits. It also places a ban on "sanctuary city" policies allowing local governments to limit cooperation between state and local law enforcement agencies and Immigration and Customs Enforcement (ICE) in the enforcement

of immigration laws. The proposed bill also requires that state and local government agencies only hire contractors who use the E-Verify system to check their workers' immigration statuses. Having passed both chambers of the state legislature, the bill has been sent for Governor Patrick McCrory's signature. The governor has not indicated whether he will sign it into law.

Los Angeles County Unveils New PEP Policy
On September 22, Los Angeles County Sheriff Jim McDonnell announced a new policy outlining how his agency will cooperate with ICE. Under the guidelines, LA County will only comply with a detainer—a request from ICE to hold a person beyond their scheduled release for transfer into ICE custody—if it meets ICE's detainer requirements and is not protected by the California Trust Act. The California Trust Act, enacted in 2013, bars law enforcement agencies in the state from honoring detainers, but does not protect those who have been convicted of serious crimes such as burglary, assault, sexual abuse, or felony DUI. ICE agents will also be allowed access to inmates in LA County jails being processed for release, as well as interview inmates who have committed serious crimes as defined by the Trust Act and have a high likelihood of being in the United States without authorization. The new policy is in response to a federal initiative called the Priority Enforcement Program (PEP), which allows ICE agents to match the fingerprints of inmates in local jails against DHS immigration databases to determine their immigration status. PEP replaced the controversial Secure Communities program in July.

Chinese Exclusion Act of 1882 Initiates Decades of Racist Immigration Policy

Doug Chin

An activist in the Seattle, Washington, Asian American community since the 1970s, writer Doug Chin has served as president of the Organization of Chinese Americans (OCA) and penned several books about the Chinese American experience.

This year marks the 130th year since the passage of the Chinese Exclusion Act of 1882. It was the first federal law that excluded immigration of a single group of people based on race. Moreover, its passage was the start of eight decades of racist immigration policies towards Asians that began with Chinese exclusion, than Japanese exclusion, and followed by severe restrictions of Filipinos.

The Chinese Exclusion Acts

The 1882 Chinese Exclusion Act prohibited (1) the immigration of Chinese laborers, (2) denied Chinese of naturalization, (3) and required Chinese laborers already legally present in the U.S. who later wish to reenter to obtain "certificates of return." The later provision was an unprecedented requirement that applied only to Chinese residents. Other Acts were passed and steps taken by the U.S. to extend the 1882 Chinese Exclusion Act. The Scott Act (1888) prohibited all Chinese laborers who would choose or had chosen to leave the U.S. from reentering and cancelled all previously issued "certificates of return," which stranded approximately 20,000 Chinese laborers abroad. The Geary Act (1892) extended the Chinese Exclusion Act for 10 years and required all Chinese persons in the U.S.—but no other race—to register with the federal government in order to obtain "certificates of residence." In 1898, the U.S. annexed Hawaii and took control

"The Chinese Exclusion Acts: A Racist Chapter in U.S. Civil Rights History," by Doug Chin, OCA Greater Seattle Chapter, May 21, 2012. Reprinted by permission.

of the Philippines, and excluded thousands of Chinese in Hawaii and the Philippines from entering the U.S. mainland.

In 1902, Congress indefinitely extended all laws relating and restricting Chinese immigration and residence, and expressly applied such laws to U.S. territories.

Anti-Chinese Era

The passage of the Chinese Exclusions Acts were extremely damaging to the early Chinese immigrants and the plight of Chinese in America. The passage of these Acts was a grave manifestation of anti-Chinese sentiment that began with the arrival of the Chinese in California in the 1850s and eventually spread throughout the American West, intensifying with the increased presence of Chinese. Along with many state and local anti-Chinese laws, these federal acts were a significant part of a vicious, violent, brutal, systematic campaign of ethnic cleansing that lasted for several decades.

Ironically, the attacks against the Chinese occurred despite the vital role they played in developing the American West. From the time they arrived and over the following three decades, these Chinese immigrants worked as domestic servants, laundrymen, miners, road graders, railroad workers, cannery workers, fishermen, cooks, farmers, and other occupations that were often shunned by whites. Their work greatly contributed to the establishment of the mining, fishing, railroad, timber and lumber, coal mining and agricultural industries in the West.

Despite their contribution in developing the western frontier, the anti-Chinese sentiment steadily grew and peaked during the 1870s and 1880s. The anti-Chinese era clearly became one of the most ferocious and outrageous display of racism in the history of the American West. Humiliating, berating, harassing, beating and murdering of Chinese were such commonplace occurrences that newspapers seldom bothered to print the stories. Among the hundreds of lynchings in the West, the majority of those lynched were Chinese. By the end of the 1880s, hundreds of towns in the West kicked-out their Chinese—either by angered mobs or legislation.

The anti-Chinese sentiment did not escape Washington state. When the first territorial legislature convened in 1853, it immediately adopted a measure to deny Chinese the right to vote, even though there were few if any Chinese living in the territory. By the mid-1860s, after a small number of Chinese began to appear in the area, territorial legislators passed additional anti-Chinese laws. One law barred Chinese from testifying against whites in court. Another measure, titled, "An Act to Protect Free White Labor Against Competition with Chinese Coolie Labor and to Discourage the Immigration of Chinese in the Territory," resulted in a poll tax levied on every Chinese. The violent anti-Chinese outbreaks in Washington reached its height in the mid-1880s with attempts to directly get rid of the Chinese at various worksites and towns in Western Washington including Newcastle, Olympia and Bellingham. Some 700 Chinese in Tacoma were removed from its Chinese quarters, which was also burned to the ground, while some 350 Chinese in Seattle were forcibly removed during this period.

The causes that led to Chinese exclusion centered on racism coupled with economic reasons. Seeing the Chinese as "unfair labor competition"—because they were willing to get paid lower wages and willing to do jobs whites shunned—was a major reason why the dominant white population wanted to exclude them. For sure, this perception was evident when economic conditions were bad and many were out of work. However, there were other reasons America wanted to exclude the Chinese. The perception of Chinese as deceitful, heathens, despotic, cruel, filthy, cowards, and intellectually inferior was prevalent among American historians, diplomats and traders. And, because of their yellow skins and their different beliefs and culture, the Chinese were seen as inassimilable. Moreover, the Chinese were thought to be unworthy of American citizenship, and even a danger to the political and social integrity of America. The Chinese in America were not only denied basic civil rights and equal protection under the law, they were denied nationalization and basically denied immigration to the U.S. for decades. The consequences of exclusion for the Chinese in America were predictable: The failure to grow in numbers as an ethnic group, minimal growth of Chinese families, illegal Chinese immigration, isolation and segregation into the Chinatowns, greater drugs and crime in Chinatowns, disappearance of Chinatowns, lack of educational and employment opportunities, separation from families and relatives in China.

The Chinese Exclusion Acts were repealed by a 1943 bill sponsored by Washington state Senator Warren Magnuson. The repeal set a quota of 105 Chinese immigrants to the U. S. annually and allowed Chinese in America to become nationalized. But, the repeal bill was passed because of the fear that the Japanese would use the Chinese Exclusion Acts as propaganda to distance its war ally, China, from the U.S. Its passage was not primarily to provide Chinese in America with basic rights nor to improve their plight.

New Chinese Immigration and Anti-Chinese Era

It was not until the passage of the 1965 Immigration Act that Chinese immigrants were allowed to immigrate to the U.S. on a large scale. Under this Act, a limit of 170,000 immigrants from the Eastern Hemisphere were allowed to enter the United States annually with a ceiling of 20,000 from each country. The changes in immigration law led to the arrival of Chinese from the People's Republic of China, Hong Kong and Taiwan as well as other Southeast Asian countries. Subsequently, Chinese immigration to the U.S. has increased so much that their population in the America has practically doubled every decade since the passage of the 1965 Act. These new immigrants arrived to an America that is much more tolerant of Chinese than that of the anti-Chinese decades, thanks in large part to the civil rights movement in the 1960s that opened up economic and educational opportunities for racial minorities and others. Since the 1970s, there are programs to help immigrants and refugees to adjust to America, to find jobs and create businesses, to further their education, and deal with legal issues.

The relative success of these new Chinese immigrants and relative absence of discrimination towards them, however, has made it difficult for them to relate to the sad and painful anti-Chinese period. For them, as well as other Chinese and Asians, the anti-Chinese era should be learned and remembered as a period when Chinese immigrants were the victims of one of the most racist attacks in American history and the ethnic group that America wanted to totally exclude. Comprehension of the Chinese Exclusion Acts and what brought them about and their impacts should bring about an appreciation for the hardship and endurance of the early Chinese immigrants. Moreover, it should inspire Chinese and other Asian Americans to continually fight for civil rights and equal treatment for all. In this context, and of immediate concern, is the struggle to ensure the rights of legal and illegal immigrants to this country and the campaign to ensure "Justice for Private Danny Chen."

Mass Deportations Are Already a Part of American History

Adrian Florido

Adrian Florido is a reporter for NPR's Code Switch team, where he covers race, identity, and culture.

Presidential candidate Donald Trump's proposal to deport all 11 million immigrants living in the country illegally, along with their U.S.-born children, sounds far-fetched. But something similar happened before.

During the 1930s and into the 1940s, up to 2 million Mexicans and Mexican-Americans were deported or expelled from cities and towns across the U.S. and shipped to Mexico. According to some estimates, more than half of these people were U.S. citizens, born in the United States.

It's a largely forgotten chapter in history that Francisco Balderrama, a California State University historian, documented in *Decade of Betrayal: Mexican Repatriation in the 1930s*. He co-wrote that book with the late historian Raymond Rodriguez.

"There was a perception in the United States that Mexicans are Mexicans," Balderrama said. "Whether they were American citizens, or whether they were Mexican nationals, in the American mind—that is, in the mind of government officials, in the mind of industry leaders—they're all Mexicans. So ship them home."

It was the Great Depression, when up to a quarter of Americans were unemployed and many believed that Mexicans were taking scarce jobs. In response, federal, state and local officials launched so-called "repatriation" campaigns. They held raids in workplaces and in public places, rounded up Mexicans and Mexican-

Americans alike, and deported them. The most famous of these was in downtown Los Angeles' Placita Olvera in 1931.

Balderrama says these raids were intended to spread fear throughout Mexican barrios and pressure Mexicans and Mexican-Americans to leave on their own. In many cases, they succeeded.

Where they didn't, government officials often used coercion to get rid of Mexican-Americans who were U.S. citizens. In Los Angeles, it was standard practice for county social workers to tell those receiving public assistance that they would lose it, and that they would be better off in Mexico. Those social workers would then get tickets for families to travel to Mexico. According to Balderrama's research, one-third of LA's Mexican population was expelled between 1929 and 1944 as a result of these practices.

That's what happened to Emilia Castañeda and her family.

Castañeda was born in Los Angeles in 1926 to immigrant parents. Her mother died while she was growing up, and her father struggled to get work during the Depression. When Castañeda was nine, Los Angeles County paid to put the family on a southbound train to Mexico. They lived with relatives, but often had to sleep outdoors for lack of space.

"The oldest of the boys, he used to call me a *repatriada*," Castañeda remembered in a 1971 interview, using the Spanish word for a repatriate. "And I don't think I felt that I was a *repatriada*, because I was an American citizen." Castañeda didn't return to the U.S. until she was 17, by which point she had lost much of her English. Her father never returned.

Balderrama says these family separations remain a lasting legacy of the mass deportations of that era. Despite claims by officials at the time that deporting U.S.-born children—along with their immigrant parents—would keep families together, many families were destroyed.

Esteban Torres was a toddler when his father, a Mexican immigrant, was caught up in a workplace roundup at an Arizona copper mine in the mid-1930s. "My mother, like other wives, waited for the husbands to come home from the mine. But he didn't come home," Torres recalled in a recent interview. He now lives east of Los Angeles. "I was 3 years old. My brother was 2 years old. And we never saw my father again."

Torres' mother suspected that his father had been targeted because of his efforts to organize miners. That led Esteban Torres to a lifelong involvement with organized labor. He was eventually elected to the U.S. House of Representatives and served there from 1983 to 1999.

Today, Torres serves on the board of La Plaza de Cultura y Artes in Los Angeles, a Mexican-American cultural center. In front of it stands a memorial that the state of California dedicated in 2012, apologizing to the hundreds of thousands of U.S. citizens who were illegally deported or expelled during the Depression.

"It was a sorrowful step that this country took," Torres said. "It was a mistake. And for Trump to suggest that we should do it again is ludicrous, stupid and incomprehensible."

Congress Condemns Chinese Exclusion Act

Ted Gong

Ted Gong is executive director of the 1882 Project Foundation and president of the DC chapter of the Chinese American Citizens Alliance.

PopVox is a web-based medium that tracks pending legislation in Congress. It allows citizens to express their opinion for or against proposed legislation. In the final weekend before the House vote on the House Resolution to condemn the 1882 Act and laws of exclusion, PopVox recorded the following user comments. Except when included in the body of message, indicators of the person's name and address were removed and replaced with the first initial of their email address.

H.Res. 683

H.Res. 282

A in North Carolina's 12th District (Jun 18)

Through grade-school, I was never taught much history of Asians in America. Countless times, my teachers have told me that "it was not relevant" or "it was not my specialty"—both excuses excluded me from learning the common history of my peoples. History is said to be the discipline of progress—knowing where we have come from, acknowledging patterns of political human behaviors, and hypothesizing what will come next so our nation's leaders can react appropriately. My parents instilled my appreciation of my Asian heritage (Chinese and Filipino), and my involvements during college helped me foster my passion for Asian American activism and political issues. At the bottom line, I am a proud and patriotic American. I seek a better life for myself and those around me. Excluding the true nature of the Chinese Exclusion Acts is a considerable slight against ALL Americans—robbing us all of the

"People Comment on Senate and House Resolutions Condemning the Chinese Exclusion Laws," by Ted Gong, 1882 Foundation, January 3, 2016. Reprinted by permission.

historic truth. History is supposed to be written by the victors. We must honor our history with truth, not illusion.

Justin Hua Davidson '11

d in Texas's 7th District (Jun 20)

I support H.Res. 683 because…it has been 130 years since the Chinese Exclusion Act was first enacted. Please support passage of this resolution. My Congress representatives are Senator John Cornyn and Senator Kay Bailey Hutchinson.

Dorothy Chow, Houston, TX

A in California's 8th District (Jun 19)

I support H.Res. 683 expressing regret for the Chinese Exclusion Act because this is a grave injustice to the Chinese people that contributed so much to our community. It's long overdue.

h in California's 17th District (Jun 18)

Safeguarding the civil rights of all the people requires constant vigilance. It must be taught to each succeeding generation! Today's youth need to know the struggles we and our parents had to contend with—restrictive housing covenants and racial immigration quotas among them.

W in California's 12th District (Jun 18)

Our country needs to take responsibility for racist actions in the past, in order to not repeat them. Currently, people who desire to immigrate to the U.S. are treated as criminals when it is our own system and exclusionary laws that have failed.

Sincerely, Wei Ming Dariotis.

L in California's 12th District (Jun 18)

If it wasn't for the repeal of the Chinese Exclusion laws during the 1940s and the lifting of the racial quotas in the 1960s, my own parents would not have been able to immigrate to the United States. Both of them met each other in the US, earned higher degrees of education, and worked to earn a comfortable living for themselves and their family. I can't imagine what my life would be like if they hadn't made their life changing decision to leave their home country. It's important for our country to acknowledge that targeting a specific group of people from coming to the United States and having equal status is wrong. The fact that this law was passed before is a stain on our country's record towards human rights. We must be willing to be honest and own up to this past mistake in order to move forward as a free society. As a proud citizen of the United States, I look to the Congress to vote yes on this resolution. Thank You!

Sincerely, Amy Lam, California CD-12

H in California's 2nd District (Jun 18)

My family have been discriminated since we came over in 1851 to Monterey, California. We never expected much but to be equal citizens in America. I was born the year that the Chinese Exclusion Act was finally repealed. The history of California is a bright and golden one; but never how the Chinese settled throughout our state. I am a fifth generation Chinese that is proud of the red, white, and blue. Please give us the credit how we help build this great Nation.

T in California's 14th District (Jun 18)

This approval is long overdue to the Chinese American. This will also serve as a warning sign for the future generation that discrimination against any race is shameful and unlawful. Everyone should be treated equally regardless of race or gender.

R in California's 10th District (Jun 18)

It's time for America to own up to its racist past, make amends, and move forward.

C in California's 8th District (Jun 18)

I support H.Res. 683 expressing regret for the Chinese Exclusion Act because part of the backlash from this act resulted in my father spending time at the Angel Island Immigration Station when he came to the U.S. in 1936 as a young boy. He would never talk about what he experienced while held there…but stories told by others left much to the imagination of what he was put through. To his dying day, he never mentioned that episode in his life. With the passage of H. Res. 683, perhaps he can now really rest in peace.

E in California's 12th District (Jun 18)

I support H.Res. 683 because of the hardships my Grandfather and my Father suffered during their time in America especially being separated from their wives. My Grandfather only spent 2 years with his wife in China and died in America, alone, never seeing his wife again. I had experienced the prejudices towards my parents when I was growing up and it was a horrible feeling to know you were not liked. My parents lived in fear for most of their lives. You can see it in their eyes. Both of my parents died old, and I was close to 40 years [when they died] because my mother was allowed to come to America after WWII and my dad was 40 when he had me. They never lived to meet my third child. With this said, please help to pass this bill because it is the right thing to do. Thank you for your help. This is greatly appreciated.

j in Arizona's 6th District (Jun 18)

I support H.Res. 683 because this was an unfortunate part of US history that we can all learn from. Congress should stand up and do the right thing and show the world that the US leads the way in recognizing wrongs that were done in the past and is not afraid to acknowledge it and learn from it. Thanks.

A in Virginia's 11th District (Jun 18)

I support H.Res. 683 because my family was a victim of the Chinese Exclusion Act. My family was denied entrance to the U.S. even though my father was an American Citizen.

u in California's 14th District (Jun 18)

It is time to apologize to Chinese Americans about the discriminatory actions of the past by the US.

a in New Mexico's 1st District (Jun 18)

The past discrimination against Chinese and other people from Asia harmed a group of citizens who have contributed selflessly to this country. My parents who emigrated in 1952 felt the effects of this discrimination when they lived in Clovis, NM, and this resolution will provide reassurance that Congress can recognize its mistakes and rectify wrongs. We look forward to your leadership and support of this resolution.

G in California's 13th District (Jun 18)

My ancestors who arrived from China by Chinese sailing junk (boat) to America in 1851 to the Monterey Peninsula, California area were affected by the Chinese Exclusion Act of 1882. My great grandmother Quock Mui is the first documented Chinese female born in the Monterey Bay Area. My ancestor's Chinese fishing village in Pacific Grove burned down mysteriously in 1906. It was this anti-Chinese climate of the time that pushed for the passing in1882 of the Chinese Exclusion Act. Please support U.S. Congress: H. Res. 683, Expressing the regret of the House of Representatives for the passage of laws that adversely affected the Chinese in the United States, including the Chinese Exclusion Act.

a in California's 14th District (Jun 18)

I support H.Res.683—and urge you to make history by putting a closure to these Chinese Exclusion Laws. Thank you.

d in Texas's 7th District (Jun 18)

It has been 130 years since the Chinese Exclusion Act was first enacted. It is time to put it behind us and move on. My Congress representatives are Senator John Cornyn and Senator Kay Bailey Hutchinson.

Daniel Chow, Houston, TX.

1 in California's 6th District (Jun 18)

I personally have family members who were prevented from immigrating to this country solely because they were Chinese. The United States has never denied entry to any other nation except the Chinese, despite the notion that "all men are created equal." The mental anguish of being separated from family directly affected my grandfather's psychic deterioration and my father's as well.

A in Oregon's 5th District (Jun 18)

My family was separated for years, with my father studying and then working for the science community in the U.S., while his family in Taiwan (Republic of China) was prevented from joining him in the U.S. due to the Immigration Quota Laws. My family in Taiwan was finally able to join my father in the U.S. in 1961, after President Kennedy signed an Executive Order allowing my family (and other families in similar situations) to wait for our Immigration Quota in the U.S. My family suffered hardship from being separated for many years.

A in Virginia's 2nd District (Jun 17)

I support H.Res. 683 because it separated members of my family beginning with my great grandfather and then my grandfather, who each came to the U.S. for better economic opportunities but could not bring their wives. My grandfather brought my father as a youth to this country in 1925 and my father ended up on his own. He stayed to make a life for himself here, but faced significant limitations under the Chinese Exclusion Act. It wasn't until 1943 when my father was drafted into the U.S. army that citizenship was finally offered to Chinese immigrants. The Act discriminated against Chinese and emerged from long-standing anti-Chinese sentiment, and justified other discriminatory actions against Chinese in America. Public recognition of the injustice of this act is important as is the promise that no group in the U.S. will ever be the target of such discriminatory legislation in the future.

A in California's 8th District (Jun 17)

Healing cannot begin without acknowledgement and recognition of the discriminatory immigration policy that singled out laborers from China. The policy had a profound effect on families, delaying the acculturation process and acceptance of Chinese in America. There are ripple effects in families even today. Regret seems too small a word for the recognition, but there must be a sincere effort to square this unjust chapter in American immigration history.

Felicia Lowe

A in Maryland's 8th District (Jun 17)

This has been an issue that has long simmered with resentment and regret and nobody has opposed this bill to make things better for all of us. It will have absolutely no negative impacts on you, other Members, or anybody in the nation. It will mean a lot to the millions of Americans who have suffered from old laws, and your contribution to passing this simple bill will renew and strengthen our faith in our Nation. Please support it and vote for it with vigor and enthusiasm!

Jim and Gale in Bethesda.

A in New York's 8th District (Jun 17)

Though I was born in the US many years after the Chinese Exclusion act was repealed, it still has a very personal impact on me—130 years after the passing of the Chinese Exclusion Act of 1882.

S in Texas's 7th District (Jun 17)

It will not cost a single penny from the Federal government and is the right thing to do.

C in New York's 3rd District (Jun 17)

Many in my family, relatives, and Chinese community suffered the adverse consequences of these laws which led to discriminatory behaviors that undermined the very humanity and integrity of all of us as people.

Jean Lau Chin

M in Washington's 7thDistrict (Jun 17)

It's the right thing to do after passing laws that were unconstitutional & adversely affected the Chinese in this country.

j in Virginia's 11th District (Jun 17)

These laws represent a shameful part of our American history that Congress must repudiate. The Chinese came here more than a century ago in search of a better life. However, they faced harsh conditions and Congress passed numerous discriminatory laws that barred the Chinese from accessing basic rights afforded to other immigrants. These laws resulted in hatred, bigotry, and prejudice towards the Chinese. Many were brutally murdered, abused, harassed, and detained. Please support passage of H. Res. 683.

B in Washington's 7th District (Jun17)

I am 70 years old—I never grew up with grandparents, aunts, uncles, cousins or any relative from my father's village in China. When my mother was able to come to Seattle with my oldest brother in 1931, they never got to return to see their family members in China again. They never were able to bring family members to reunite in the USA. My oldest brother is Wing Luke. There is a Pan-Asian American museum named after him in Seattle because he helped make huge gains in social justice, historic and cultural preservation and ethical politics. The museum has become world renowned, is a Smithsonian Affiliate and the only Pan-Asian American museum in the nation and the world. How many other "Wing Lukes" were prevented from coming to the USA by the unconstitutional 1882 Chinese Exclusion Laws that existed for 60 years? Many lost opportunities to make this country a better place. The Exclusion Laws still strike echoes of loss in my heart today.

B in California's 14th District (Jun 17)
I support H.Res. 683 because going through Angel Island Museum is still a shock to Chinese today.

A in New York's 11th District (Jun 16)
The country should take responsibility for wrongs of the past and show the Chinese community of today that it is a valued part of the citizenry. Congress should take a strong stand against discrimination of any kind.

R in New York's 17th District (Jun 16)
I support H.Res. 282, a formal apology from Congress for the Chinese Exclusion Act, which discriminated against Chinese trying to immigrate to the United States. Chinese were THE ONLY NATIONALITY SPECIFICALLY EXCLUDED from immigrating to this country. The first step to eliminating racism must always be admitting it exists. My two adopted Chinese daughters will thank you.

C in New Mexico's 1st District (Jun 16)

There were residual effects on Americans of Chinese descent well into the 1960s. The first in my family to graduate from college, I could not apply for a teaching certificate and had to move to another state to provide the benefits of my education to students. My mother, an American citizen, did not vote because of intimidation at the polls. In order to vote, I had to pass a written exam on the Constitution of the United States. I vowed to help make changes in our society. State laws enabled discrimination of Chinese and other minorities, limiting housing, educational, and job opportunities. Despite these injustices, resourceful, resilient Chinese worked hard in small business enterprises, raising their children as loyal Americans embracing and serving their communities and nation. Passage of H. Res. 683 one day after Father's Day honors our forebearers for their sacrifices and their contributions. We must pledge to vigilantly avoid making the same mistakes in our shared future. This is a proud moment for all Americans who treasure justice and equality!

T in New Mexico's 1st District (Jun 16)

I am Chinese-American, and I am 80 this year. I remember how those laws, not repealed until 1943, affected my family. How we could not own land, how we were only able to live in certain areas of cities, not because we didn't have the monetary means, but because of our race. When I moved to New Mexico in 1958, the Alien Land Law, adopted into the State's Constitution in 1921, was still on the books. This law prohibited Chinese and Americans of Chinese Descent from owning land in New Mexico. After the repeal of the Chinese Exclusion Act in 1943 this rendered the New Mexico Law dead. However, this dead law was not removed until 2006, with the help of State Senator Cisco McSorley, and an informative Op-Ed by Dr. David Hsi, then President of the Albuquerque Chapter of the Chinese American Citizens Alliance. This Expression of Regret goes a long way to heal the wounds caused by these racist laws, conducted by the Congress of the past. Institutional racism has no place in the modern world. This is a great companion to Senate Res 201.

S in New Mexico's 1st District (Jun 16)

It was/is wrong to discriminate individuals based on one's race, national origin, or other personal traits and thus there should be a Congressional expression of regrets for the discriminatory laws, including the Chinese Exclusion Act of 1882, against Chinese immigrants in the 20th century.

p in California's 13th District (Jun 16)

As a Chinese American, I believe the past unfair treatment of Chinese should be officially recognized by the US government. It's humanity. Thank you.

3 in Virginia's 11th District (Jun 16)

While not the apology that it should be, H.Res. 683 is an historic act by Congress that brings attention to its role in the shameful Chinese Exclusion Laws. The resolution ensures that this history is not forgotten. This awareness then forces us to ask for ourselves and children how did these laws, with all its violent consequences to countless individuals and families and to American Principles, get passed. The laws were not a single act explainable by an attack or calamity. They were a series of laws deliberately passed and enacted in increasing harshness over almost a century, by democratically elected and empowered officials. This resolution challenges us to understand how our democratic country got it so wrong. But, it also allows us to reaffirm our faith in a government that can evaluate its past against renewed commitments to our founding and constitutional principles, and admit wrong. This then strengthens the United States going forward, and it honors those people (Chinese or others) who suffered and struggled for the United States because they deemed this nation worth it despite exclusion laws.

J in Tennessee's 3rd District (Jun 15)

I am an ethnic Chinese who strongly feels that the US government owes an apology for the mistreatment of ethnic Chinese in the past.

R in New Mexico's 1st District (Jun 14)

There does need to be acknowledgement from both houses of congress that their predecessors did in fact do something exceptionally wrong by singling out the Chinese and Chinese Americans for unequal treatment. The Senate passed 201 last year, and the House needs to pass its own version to correct this wrong. So Chinese Americans can point to this and say, "this deserves more than just a paragraph in the History Books we teach our children. Even the contemporary Congress says what their predecessors did was wrong." To be against this bill, is to be on the wrong side of history. It is to be in the same, antiquated side as separate but equal, slavery, and internment.

A in California's 17th District (Jun 13)

My father came to America when he was very young and passed through Angel Island in San Francisco. He came to the Salinas Valley and met my mother. Although you cannot change the past, you can acknowledge the wrong this government has done as you have with the Japanese Americans.

C in Wisconsin's 4th District (Jun 12)

This will give needed closure to another ugly chapter in America's history. American laws invoked blatant and blind racism against Chinese immigrants like my grandfather and parents. Unquestionably, forgiveness and expressing regret are overdue. Please actively support, and help pass H.Res. 683.

d in New York's 14th District (Jun 12)

It would bring closure on a disgraceful part of this country's history.

r in Oregon's 1st District (Jun 12)

It's vitally important to honor those who came before us by affirming that everyone in the USA is entitled to his/her civil rights and civil liberties.

A in Texas's 18th District (Jun 12)

I was born in Greenville, MS on June 3, 1939. We couldn't go to school with the whites until 1948. I could not join the YMCA because of being Chinese. I volunteered for the USAF in 1957 and served our country proudly. After honorably discharged I graduated from Miss State Univ (without any GI Bill) and worked for Delta Air Lines for 28 years as Reservations Supervisor. I participated in early Viet Nam operations and am a life member of VFW Post 8790 and past commander of American Legion Post 590 in Houston, TX. I am on the Veterans Cemetery Council of Greater Houston and help the vets whenever I can. I love the USA and Vote regularly. The Asians have overcome many prejudices and have become great US citizens and are due the support of H Res. 683. We are not asking for any compensation, just an apology. Thank you for your time and hope for your support for this passage of H Res 683.

Sincerely, Jefferson Hong

A in Oregon's 1st District (Jun 12)

Personally, my family was impacted by those laws. My siblings and I never got to know our grandfather, a direct result of the Chinese Exclusion Act of 1882 and a series of laws that were passed and enacted since that time. My grandfather immigrated to the United States in the late 1800s. He was unable to bring his wife to be with him and instead, he made trips to China as often as possible. Those trips resulted in three sons of whom my father was the youngest. In essence, those laws separated our family from each other for years. Moreover, a visit to an underground museum in Pendleton, Oregon shows the adversity that the Chinese community suffered due to discrimination supported by those laws. As an American citizen and your constituent, I beseech you to support House Resolution 683. For more information on the resolution, please contact Allison Rose in Representative Chu's office and Brian Looser in Representative Judy Biggert's office. Thank you for considering this request.

A in Arizona's 5th District (Jun 12)

This law is the only one passed by Congress that expressly singles out and discriminates against an ethnic group. Chinese people have contributed greatly to America in the arts, science, and culture. After more than a hundred years it is time to erase this black mark on America's history.

A in Virginia's 10th District (Jun 12)

It was the only US legislation that explicitly discriminated against a people in this land of the free. The US has no moral standing to speak or stand on as a world leader of justice and human rights if it is not corrected. The Chinese Exclusion Act and related laws were wrong and shameful as a part of this great nation. Take a look at the census data from1860 to 1960 and understand how devastating these laws were to the Chinese, Asians, and America. Expressing regret is the minimal action that the Congress can take. Please act now and support and pass this resolution!

N in California's 14th District

This is long overdue. Chinese were specifically singled out for discrimination in the Exclusion laws. My great-grandfather came to the US to work on the transcontinental railroad in the 1880s at great personal peril, yet I don't think that he ever felt accepted in this country. All of his children were born in China because my great grandmother was never allowed to immigrate as a result of the Exclusion laws. His children nevertheless made their way to the US, and I believe that his grandchildren and descendants have contributed much to the American fabric—not the least of which was in the armed services. More important than an apology for the actions of the past leaders of this nation, is a recognition that this type of action should never be allowed to happen again. Thank you for your vote to support H.Res. 683.

E in Texas's 7th District (Jun 12)

The passage of the Chinese Exclusion Acts perpetrated a gross injustice to the many Chinese and Chinese Americans who lived in this country during those years without the basic civil rights and access to citizenship that robbed many of their dreams. The harm has been witnessed and now documented in many journals of Chinese Americans experiences.

A in New York's 1st District (May 5)

As an American of Chinese descent and a professor of Diversity at Stony Brook University, I support H.Res. 282.

A in Texas's 21st District (May 3)

The suffering of those people needs to be acknowledged.

A in California's 12th District (May 2)

Dear Congressperson and Senators of the US Congress. I support H.Res. 282 because it is not only a gross injustice left over from a bygone era, but it is something my children needs to see has been changed so they can grow up in an America where they can pursue their dreams and achieve their full potential without fear of racism or separatism. The US needs to show the world that as the beacon of freedom and respect for individual rights, we recognize past mistakes and are willing to admit and rectify them, and to provide no cause for other countries to pass or preserve similar antiquated and irrelevant legislation. Thank you so much for your service to the country and rectifying this hateful and divisive language in our global family.

A in California's 14th District (May 2)

I support H.Res. 282 because the US government excluded Chinese in the past, and by this action alone, we telegraphed to all Americans that it is acceptable to discriminate against people of Chinese ethnic heritage. This is not acceptable. By apologizing now, the US govt has the opportunity to tell all Americans that it is very, very important to treat people from all ethnic heritages with respect.

Larry Chang, President, Ascend Leadership.

A in New Jersey's 7th District (May 1)

I support H.Res. 282 because at no time in America's history has a group been so isolated and ostracized without reproach. Additionally, this same group has been responsible for numerous contributions to this great country including the railroads, countless innovations and inventions—in technology, the medical fields, and numerous others. This resolution is key to ensure transparency and also send a message for diversity and leadership....as this country has been built on the ideals and diversity of its people.

A in Missouri's 9th District(May 1)

I support H.Res. 282 because it is a moral obligation to right the wrong.

A in New Jersey's 8th District (May 1)

As author of "Closing the Gate: Race, Politics, and the Chinese Exclusion Act," I fully support passage of H.Res. 282, expressing regret for passage of this racist law against Chinese immigrants. The Chinese Exclusion Act of 1882, which barred practically all Chinese from American shores, was the first federal law that banned a group of immigrants solely on the basis of race or nationality. By changing America's traditional policy of open immigration, this landmark legislation set a precedent for future restrictions against Asian immigrants in the early 1900s and against Europeans in the

1920s. Few laws have had more serious and tragic consequences in American history.

A in Mississippi's 2nd District (Apr 29)

I grew up in a town that was prejudiced against the Asians. During the 1940s I had to attend a one-room schoolhouse. A Caucasian teacher was assigned to teach 30 students. She had to make her rounds with each grade level. With the help of the Caucasian minister and some leaders in my town my people were allowed to attend the public schools. There are other incidents where my people were looked down on at that time. I won't go into this matter. Please give your support to the House Resolution 282. The Asians are asking only for an apology that this incident happened. I appreciate your time and your support.

A in Virginia's 8th District (Apr 29)

Discrimination continues to this day. An important step in ending this discrimination is by enacting laws that demonstrate our government's commitment to democracy for all. The federal government has addressed the wrongs of the Japanese internment camps during WWII. The federal government has addressed the wrongs done to the African Americans. Now it's time to address the wrongs done to the Chinese Americans. One of the things that makes America great is that America recognizes its mistakes and tries to correct them. Don't make the same mistake twice by ignoring the passage of resolution 282. I am a 3rd generation American born Chinese. My parents experienced, firsthand, the devastating affect this discriminatory act had on countless individuals and families for generations. My own life has been scarred by overt & subtle racism since childhood, and I know my experience is not unique among other Chinese Americans. Mr. Moran, you have the power to cast an uncontroversial vote that will improve the future of society. Vote yes to 282.

A in Maryland's 8th District (Apr 28)

I support H.Res. 282 because most Americans are unaware of how the U.S. historically has treated people who came from China.

A in New Jersey's 5th District (Apr 28)

I support H.Res. 282 ("Expressing the regret of the House of Representatives for the passage of discriminatory laws against") because…It is illegal to have such law under the US constitution.

A in Oregon's 3rd District (Apr 27)

I support H.Res. 282 because it is long overdue. The Chinese community has been instrumental in shaping U.S. history but not given the due credit and recognition in the history books.

A in California's 10th District (Apr 26)

I support H.Res. 282 because we should not have any race discrimination.

A in Oregon's 5th District (Apr 26)

My great-grandfather who immigrated in the 1800s to Portland and was a Chinese merchant in the original Chinatown south of Burnside…my grandfather who brought my grandmother and father here from southern China in 1931…they all suffered the brunt of America's anti-Chinese laws and racial discrimination. This is a step in the right direction towards the healing of a nation. I respectfully request that you lend your support to the passage of H.Res. 282. I sincerely thank you for your time.

A in New Jersey's 4th District (Apr 26)

As an American-born citizen of Chinese descent, I have a "basic right" in accordance with the principles upon which America was founded to make a "simple" non-partisan request "to right a wrong." Why is it so difficult in today's society and times for Congress to pass this bill? My parents are no longer alive but they as well as my entire family would be proud and happy that Congress can finally face up to the facts regarding the passage of the unjust discriminatory laws and express its regrets to an important part of its constituencies. This is especially important to me personally because I am currently the President of the New Jersey Chapter of OCA (Organization of Chinese Americans). OCA is a national 501(c)(3) advocacy organization headquartered in Washington, DC.

A in California's 3rd District (Apr 26)

I support H.Res. 282 because it's unconstitutional.

j in Minnesota's 5th District (Apr 26)

These past laws have left an immediate legacy in present-day issues of race and immigration. Our history of exclusion reminds us that the United States has only in recent decades moved closer to its promise of being a truly free and equal society. As the daughter of immigrants from China, I am well aware that my identity as an American would have been questioned (not just culturally, but legally) at one point in time; as an American, I feel that it is only by acknowledging the true history that we can make progress as a nation. I do hope you will give this resolution your full support.

A in Maryland's 8th District (Apr 26)

I support H.Res. 282 because it's time (actually long passed) to right this wrong.

A in California's 9th District

Not only did this Exclusion Act discriminate against Chinese, but subsequently the law included Japanese.

A in Virginia's 2nd District (Apr 25)

The exclusion laws against Chinese immigrants sentenced at least a whole generation of these people to a life of limited economic, educational, and social opportunities and marginal legal status. For decades these laws prevented Chinese from owning property and becoming citizens. With the U.S. government's '"lawful" unequal treatment of Chinese immigrants, this immigrant group became easy targets of discrimination and violence from many sources and had little recourse. Three generations of my father's family came to America from China for better opportunities, but only my father stayed—enduring the law's restrictions for 18 years before being drafted into the U.S. Army. Only then in 1943 were drafted immigrants allowed to become citizens, which made sense if they were expected to fight for America. Chinese immigrants have contributed to America's success in many ways over the last two centuries, and it is time for the government to acknowledge that these exclusion acts were unjust and discriminatory against the Chinese.

A in Illinois's 10th District (Apr 25)

It will right the wrong this country did more than a hundred years ago. More important, it will educate all the people about the history. That will strengthen the relationship among all the races of US citizens. Your action on this will be appreciated.

A in California's 17th District (Apr 25)

I believe America should own up to its mistakes and apologize for the wrongs that were committed against Chinese immigrants because of the Chinese Exclusion Act of 1882. Saying "sorry" is just the beginning. Funds should be allocated to inform and educate Americans about the contributions of immigrants to this nation and the negative impact of unfair immigration policies on individuals, families, communities, and this nation so that we can move forward and not repeat mistakes of the past. As President Obama put it in his major address on immigration reform, America is a nation of immigrants and a nation of laws. I urge you to support H.Res. 282 and comprehensive immigration reform.

A in Oregon's 3rd District (Apr 25)

I support H.Res. 282 because people have failed to recognize the great contribution of early Chinese laborers & immigrants in building the West.

A in Maryland's 8th District (Apr 25)

The time has come for our country and congress to express regrets for past discriminatory actions and embrace a new multicultural society that is working hard to make this great nation achieve even higher goals of national integration.

A in Maryland's 8th District (Apr 25)

It is important to me that our country rights past wrongs and always continues to uphold liberty and freedom for all.

A in Maryland's 8th District (Apr 25)

The injustice done to the Chinese American community needed to be recognized by the larger American community.

A in Colorado's 3rd District (Apr 25)

I am a member of the Chinese American Citizens Alliance and my family was directly impacted by these unjust set of laws collectively known as the Chinese Exclusion Act.

A in California's 6th District (Apr 21)

These laws created great suffering and hardship for my Chinese ancestors just because of their race.

J in California's 40th District (Apr 19)

The Chinese Exclusion Act was grossly unfair and caused profound and long lasting harm to the Chinese population in the U.S. I have relatives, including my parents, and numerous acquaintances who made positive contributions to their communities but suffered the fear of deportation for decades. An apology from the U.S. government cannot undo all the harm, but it is still an important, and one of no financial cost, gesture of good will that would help the Chinese communities feel that a long overdue reconciliation effort is being made.

a in Virginia's 8th District (Apr 19)

My grandparents came over from mainland China in the 1920s and settled in Baltimore, MD, and my grandparents were subjected to this act. I am the vice president of the Chinese American Citizens Alliance D.C. Lodge. I have lived in Arlington, VA, since 1996.

   Alex Lee

A in Texas's 18th District (Apr 15)

I was born in Greenville, MS, Jun 1939. Was not able to attend a white or mixed race school until 1947. Mother was born in Rosedale, MS, in 1916 and was part of the law suit filed by my great aunt in 1923, *LumGong verses Rice* for my Aunt's daughters to attend a white school. Case lost in the MS state and Federal Supreme courts. I am a USAF veteran and served in 1957–61 as well as another brother in USAF and baby brother in USMC in Vietnam. Please pass H.Res.282 with no exceptions. I am a past commander and an American Legion Lifetime member of VFW post 8790 and an officer on the VA Cemetery Council of Greater Houston. We all are Loyal and law abiding citizens of this great country. And all my family are regular voters. Thanks for your vote.

A in California's 40th District (Apr 14)

I grew up in the MS Delta and was not able to attend public school until the 3th grade due to being Chinese. My father and a number of other Chinese families started a Baptist Mission school for teaching English and Math to Chinese students until the mid-forties when the school in my home town finally allowed my brothers and I to attend public school. Due to the 1882 Exclusion Act, my father and mother were not allowed to become US Citizens until the 1950s although they had worked in the United States from 1917 and paid taxes running a small Mom and Pop grocery store.

M in Arizona's 7th District (Apr 10)

Because it corrects a seriously wrongful act, because such a rectification is a healing step for our Nation, because it is not an act fostering monetary claims against the treasury, because my parents were only able to reunite and have our family of four here in Arizona because Father was an Army Air Force veteran of WWII, so I might not be here today had error persisted.

e in Texas's 1st District (Mar 29)

I have witnessed the pride and patriotism of Good and Loyal American Citizens of Chinese descent.

t in California's 35th District (Mar 25)

As a Chinese American, I live in a society that still discriminates against Americans with Chinese heritage. Though I was brought up as an American, I am still viewed by many as too Asian because of my Chinese heritage. I believe that an apology is the first step to healing and easing tensions between Congress and the Chinese American community. If the Japanese American community was given an official apology by United States Executive Order 9066 to all persons of Japanese ancestry, the Chinese Americans should be given the same because of the 1882 Chinese Exclusion Act. I recommend this to show that healing has begun.

A in Texas's 21st District (Mar 21)

It took twenty years for me to learn about the wrong that our glorious country had once done to the people of my ethnicity. However, it's unfortunate that I had to enroll into an Asian American History course at the University of Texas to learn about the oppression, discrimination, miscegenation, and segregation laws that were enacted by congress in the early 1900s because Caucasians felt threatened by Asian immigration into this country. Although the people of my Vietnamese race didn't immigrate into the US until 1975 and did not have to endure through these racist regulations like other Asian Americans before us, it was the laws like the Chinese Exclusion Act during the late 1800s that set precedent for the same discrimination that was brought towards the Japanese, Koreans, and Punjabis that immigrated into the US during the early 1900s up until World War 2. Their stories and struggles are a part of our history because these early immigrants contributed so much to the early growth of THIS nation because of their labor, yet an apology for their mistreatment has not been made even after a CENTURY. There needs to be more awareness, and it starts with this resolution in congress!

A in Texas's 25th District (Mar19)

Passage of H.Res. 282 would promote greater awareness and understanding of America's troubled history of immigration restriction. Much of the problems we currently experience in deciding whose entry is restricted and how, and who has rights to permanent settlement, as well as the difficulties in enforcing these preferences, stem from the initial efforts to legislate and to implement the Chinese exclusion laws. This legislation targeted Chinese as a race, which de facto cast doubt on the presence of all Chinese present in the US as undocumented individuals. In part, Chinese broke the laws because they regarded them as unfair and unrecognizing of the ambition and drive of Chinese immigrants to work hard to their own benefit but also for that of the US. This troubled history can inform and help Americans make decisions about immigration restriction and enforcement that will produce more functional laws and bureaucracy to enforce them.

b in Virginia's 11th District (Mar 4)

The Chinese Exclusion Act was an injustice to the Chinese and all Asians who were included in subsequent exclusionary laws. It distorted our family's lives. My family and all other Chinese families we knew lived in fear as I grew up in Detroit, Michigan before, during, and after World War II. HRES. 282 is a testament that Congress repudiates racially based exclusion and endorses the national heritages of all Americans.

Mexican Repatriation Is a Part of Texas History

Robert R. McKay

Historian Robert R. McKay is a contributor to the Texas State Historical Association's Handbook of Texas Online.

Mexican Americans and Repatriation

Although a great deal of attention has been focused on Mexican immigration by scholars on both sides of the border, far less attention has been given to emigration of Mexicans and Mexican Americans from the United States. Casual reference has been made in many studies to the repatriation of Mexicans from Texas, but few published studies have examined these departures in detail. The most neglected era of Mexican repatriation from the United States is before 1930. Although substantial Mexican repatriation from Texas occurred at that time, no published study has examined Mexican departures between 1836 and 1930. Mexican repatriation during the Great Depression has received more attention. During the 1930s, a single article on Mexican repatriation from Texas was published; "The Mexicans Go Home" by Edna E. Kelley appeared in the *Southwest Review* in 1932. Nothing more appeared until the 1980s, when four brief articles on diverse aspects of depression-era repatriation appeared. These included articles on deportation from the lower Rio Grande valley (1981), on Mexican repatriation and the Texas Cotton Acreage Control Law of 1931–32 (1983), on the repatriation of Bridgeport, Texas, coal miners (1984), and on Mexican repatriation from South Texas (1990).

Mexican repatriation from Texas is often associated with the Great Depression of the 1930s because of the massive exodus that occurred during that time. Large numbers of Mexicans were repatriated from Texas before that time, however. The departures began soon after Texas declared its independence from Mexico.

"Mexican Americans and Repatriation," by Robert R. McKay, Texas State Historical Association, June 15, 2010. Reprinted by permission.

Much of this cross-border migration was associated with the seasonal return of Mexican labor to Mexico each fall. However, exceptionally large numbers of Mexicans were compelled to return to Mexico periodically. Perhaps the first large-scale repatriation occurred at the conclusion of the Mexican War in 1848. San Antonio, for example, was practically abandoned by Mexicans after 1848, and a number of Mexicans were repatriated under the sponsorship of the Mexican government in the late 1840s. The precise number of Mexicans returned to Mexico from Texas during this period is unknown, although they probably numbered several thousand. During the remainder of the nineteenth century, harassment against Mexicans by Anglo-Americans was occasionally so severe that many were forced to abandon their homes in Texas and return to Mexico. In the 1850s a number of Mexicans were driven from their homes in Central Texas, and in 1856 the entire Mexican population of Colorado County was reportedly ordered to leave the county. Conflict between Anglo-Americans and Mexicans in the 1870s reportedly resulted in the expulsion of Mexicans from various locations in South Texas.

The first mass Mexican repatriation movement from Texas during the twentieth century occurred in 1915 and was an indirect result of efforts by Mexicans to implement the irredentist "Plan of San Diego." Although the plan consisted of fifteen specific points, its fundamental objective was to organize the Mexican people of the Southwest and encourage them to rebel against United States authority and reconquer territories lost by Mexico to the United States in the nineteenth century. Mexican efforts to implement the plan resulted in numerous well-organized raids against the Texas Rangers, local posses, and the United States Army in the lower Rio Grande valley beginning in July. The panic that gripped Anglo-American society in the Valley after July 1915 resulted in widespread harassment and intimidation of the Mexican population of Texas. Fear among Valley residents changed to hysteria in September as the border raids increased. Anglo-American fear and vengeance proved to be effective in intimidating Mexican residents, as evidenced by the forced repatriation of thousands of Mexicans. By mid-September the repatriation movement became a massive exodus, as the roads leading to the border were congested with lengthy wagontrains of fleeing Mexicans. As many as one-half of the Mexican residents of the lower Rio Grande valley abandoned their homes in 1915, although the precise number has not been established. Following on the heels of the 1915 exodus, significant numbers of Mexicans felt compelled to abandon their Texas homes during World War I. Although the demand for labor in Texas remained strong throughout the war, many Mexicans periodically returned to Mexico because of fear of conscription into the United States military and because of widespread misunderstanding regarding the selective-service legislation adopted in May 1917. This legislation required all men, including aliens, between twenty-one and thirty-one years of age to register for military service. Mexican residents of Texas could not understand why they were required to register for military service if they were not subject to the draft; consequently, thousands left their homes in Texas for Mexico.

Nevertheless, the number of repatriates was minuscule compared to those who returned to Mexico during the Great Depression. With the deterioration of the United States economy after 1929, between 400,000 and 500,000 Mexicans and their American-born children returned to Mexico. More than half of these departed from Texas. (The term *Mexican* is used in this article to refer to all Mexican-heritage repatriates, although a significant number of them were Mexican Americans since they had been born in Texas. For Mexican Americans, the term *repatriate* is actually inaccurate, for one cannot be repatriated to a foreign country.) Depression-era Mexican repatriation from Texas began in 1929, gained momentum in 1930, and peaked in 1931. In the last quarter of 1931 repatriation reached massive proportions; the roads leading to the Texas-Mexico border became congested with returning repatriates. Mexican border towns were also crowded as thousands of returning Mexicans awaited transportation to the interior of Mexico. The number of repatriates declined in 1932 and again in 1933. During the middle years of the depression—1934 to 1938—only occasional groups of repatriates left Texas. Then in 1939 and continuing into 1940, a significant number of Mexicans were repatriated from the state by the Mexican government.

Most Texas repatriation after 1929 originated in five areas. Most of the numerous repatriates of the lower Rio Grande valley had been employed as laborers on large truck farms, although some had worked in packing plants and other agribusinesses. Repatriation from some Valley towns was so complete that few Mexicans remained. South Texas probably furnished the second-largest number of repatriates. They departed from hundreds of cotton plantations and farms where they had served as tenant farmers and laborers. Third, many rural communities and small towns throughout Central Texas furnished repatriates. These had been employed as tenant farmers and laborers on large cotton plantations and as unskilled laborers in cotton-related industries. Fourth, significant numbers of repatriates left Southwest Texas. These had been employed on the cattle and sheep ranches and as agricultural laborers in the Winter Garden region. Fifth, West Texas was a source of repatriation. From the extensive cotton farms on the South Plains to the silver mines in the Big Bend, Mexicans departed en masse.

Although most Mexicans were repatriated from rural areas of Texas, a substantial number returned to Mexico from urban centers. At least some departed from every large Texas city, but the largest number departed from San Antonio, El Paso, Houston, and Dallas-Fort Worth. Many urban repatriates had been employed as seasonal or permanent workers in labor-intensive industries before the depression curtailed employment. Mexicans were among the first discharged. Many urban Mexicans initially refused to abandon their homes in Texas; only after their savings were exhausted did they reluctantly return to Mexico. Urban repatriation was fueled by intense local anti-Mexican campaigns as well as by a statewide Immigration Service deportation campaign. Owners of small commercial enterprises, artisans, and professional persons were severely harmed by the depression. Their financial problems were compounded by the repatriation or deportation of thousands of customers. The effects of the depression on Mexican businesses was perhaps greatest at El Paso, where hundreds of commercial enterprises closed. Many of the owners were compelled to return to Mexico. Many repatriates returned to Mexico in good financial condition and in their own vehicles, laden with farm equipment, tools, livestock, furniture, merchandise, household goods, and other belongings. However, the possession of material belongings was not always an indication of financial wellbeing. Rural repatriates who returned with substantial belongings frequently lacked money to begin life as farmers in Mexico. Urban entrepreneurs often left with merchandise so they could reestablish their businesses, yet they usually lacked funds to do so once they reached Mexico. The repatriates' belongings were often of such little monetary value that they were unable to sell them. Repatriates who owned vehicles frequently could not pay to acquire license plates, oil, gasoline, and tires, or to make repairs.

Perhaps the most important cause of the repatriation of Mexicans from Texas in the 1930s was the deterioration of the agricultural economy of Texas, since most Texas repatriates had been employed as tenant farmers and agricultural laborers. Mexican farmworkers were devastated by declining wages after 1929. For example, the average wage paid cottonpickers decreased from $1.21 per 100 pounds of cotton picked in 1928 to forty-four cents in 1931. Mexican laborers simply could not live on such low wages. State and federal legislation designed to mitigate the impact of the depression on the poor also contributed to the repatriation of thousands of Mexicans. Two of the most important laws were the Texas Cotton Acreage Control Law of 1931–32 and the Agricultural Adjustment Act of 1933, which caused the displacement of large numbers of Mexicans in the early depression. In response to both laws, landlords evicted thousands of Mexican tenant farmers and agricultural laborers who subsequently returned to Mexico. Similarly, federal legislation systematically excluded alien employment on federal work-relief projects. In virtually all Texas communities Mexicans were denied work because of these federal provisions. Mexican Americans who were unable to prove their citizenship were routinely denied employment. The denial of relief work on Civil Works Administration and Work Projects Administration projects was especially devastating to Mexicans because these projects provided a major source of employment for unskilled labor during the depression. State requirements limited the employment of Mexicans on state-financed public-works projects. Employment was denied to them in state highway construction and maintenance, in construction of state buildings, and in teaching at public schools. Before 1930 construction projects had provided a major source of employment for semiskilled and unskilled Mexican labor. Many municipal and county governments adopted ordinances and resolutions that required the employment of local labor on locally financed projects. Mexicans were often denied employment because these ordinances usually had lengthy citizenship requirements that they could not meet. In addition, informal regulations were often used to deny relief to Mexicans. Local communities sometimes denied relief and employment to Mexicans who temporarily left home to engage in seasonal agricultural work because they had not been continuous residents.

Repatriation was accompanied by a federal deportation campaign that began in 1928 and intensified between 1929 and 1931. Deportation raids were carried out in both urban and rural areas. The most intense activity was conducted near the Texas-Mexico border. Few massive deportation raids were staged in Texas after 1931, although Immigration Service inspectors apprehended and deported Mexicans throughout the 1930s. Deportation raids received widespread publicity in Texas. Threat of deportation led to the exodus of thousands of Texas residents, including many Mexicans residing legally in the state. The deportation campaign began in the lower Rio Grande valley in the summer of 1928 and continued through 1931, when thousands of Mexicans were jailed and deported. The campaign was so thorough that in some small rural communities few or no Mexicans remained after 1931. By 1930 the campaign had been extended to West Texas, where activity centered on El Paso and nearby agricultural enterprises. Thousands were deported, and authorities in Ciudad Juárez had great difficulty in providing for their needs. The campaign was less intense in other areas of Texas, although raids occurred at diverse locations in South, Central, and North Texas. Reliable data are not available for the number of deportations from the various areas of the state. Efforts to implement the deportation campaign resulted in widespread violation of civil and human rights, including illegally imprisoning immigrants, deporting United States-born children, not permitting returnees to dispose of their property or to collect their wages, deporting many not legally subject to deportation because of their length of Texas residence, separating families, and deporting the infirm.

A number of institutions were involved in Mexican repatriation from Texas during the Great Depression. Perhaps the most important of these was the Mexican government, which promoted repatriation from Texas by reducing import tariffs on the repatriates' belongings and offering free transportation from the border. Reduction of import duties was an influential factor for long-term Texas residents who had accumulated many belongings, while free transportation was important to destitute repatriates. Mexican consuls in Texas encouraged repatriation as official government policy. Consuls served as the major communication link between prospective repatriates in the state and the Mexican government, and they provided information on opportunities in Mexico. Although they had limited money to aid needy repatriates, consuls often led drives to raise funds to transport repatriates from Texas. Further, they often initiated, organized, and implemented the return of repatriates. The Mexican consuls organized chapters of the Comisión Honorífica Mexicana, quasi-official bodies that served as their extensions in local communities. The comisiones provided information regarding opportunities in Mexico to prospective repatriates. They then offered organizational expertise to those who decided to return. In addition, they assisted in raising money to transport repatriates from their homes to the border. Several other Mexican government agencies assisted in repatriation. The presidents, through a series of decrees, abolished import duties on repatriates' belongings. The Ministry of Interior provided destitute repatriates with transportation from the border to their destinations in Mexico. The Mexican Migration Service expedited the passage of the repatriates through border communities and often organized drives to raise funds for them. During the late depression the Ministry of Foreign Relations recruited Texas Mexicans to colonize land in Mexico. Social organizations also played an important role. These included sociedades mutualistas, social clubs, patriotic societies, and Comités pro-Repatriados. They raised funds to return Mexicans to the border and provided other financial and material assistance.

The specific destinations of most repatriates are unknown. Apparently most returned to the towns and villages from which they had emigrated, although some went to urban centers and government-sponsored agricultural colonies. Many returned to the northern border states of Nuevo León, Coahuila, Tamaulipas, and Chihuahua, while a somewhat smaller number returned to Guanajuato, San Luis Potosí, Michoacán, Jalisco, Durango, Zacatecas, and Aguascalientes, in central Mexico. Large-scale efforts were made to provide returnees with land to farm. Land was made available for colonization projects by the National Irrigation Commission, other federal agencies, state agencies, and individuals. Most repatriates were resettled by the NIC, although many smaller projects were developed by an assortment of federal and state agencies. A few individual landowners were involved in resettlement, but few repatriates benefited from their schemes. Many of the repatriate colonies were located in northern Mexico, where large tracts of unsettled land were available. Resettlement projects in other areas of Mexico were often located in remote regions, usually on haciendas abandoned during the Mexican Revolution or on recently expropriated land. Much of the resettlement land was undeveloped; it required clearing and preparing before being cultivated. Most Texas repatriates who were resettled in Mexico went to one of six agricultural colonies in northern Mexico, all initiated by the National Irrigation Commission. These were the Don Martín, San Carlos, El Nogal, El Mante, Bajo Río San Juan, and Bajo Río Bravo. Other Mexican government agencies, state governments, and even some individuals established colonization projects designed to accommodate returning repatriates. Little information is available on the success or failure of most colonies, although some are known to have failed. Some repatriates settled at several projects before finding a successful one. Other colonists left the resettlement colonies for urban centers in search of jobs, while still others tried to reenter the United States. Displaced colonists often suffered severe hardships from these dislocations. In some cases they had to dispose of all their belongings in order to obtain travel funds.

Have Deportation and Immigration Policies Gotten Worse in the New Millennium?

Overview: President Obama's Ambivalent Record on Immigration

Jessica Bolter, Muzaffar Chishti, and Sarah Pierce

Jessica Bolter is a research assistant at Migration Policy Institute, where she provides research support to the US Immigration Policy Program. Muzaffar Chishti is director of MPI's office at New York University School of Law. Sarah Pierce is an associate policy analyst with the US Immigration Policy Program at MPI.

Barack Obama was famously labeled "deporter in chief" by critics in the immigrant-rights community, even as enforcement-first advocates accused his administration of being soft on unauthorized immigrants. Which perception is accurate? With the Obama presidency just ended, a closer examination demonstrates the administration's record is more nuanced than either criticism would imply.

Carefully calibrated revisions to Department of Homeland Security (DHS) immigration enforcement priorities and practices achieved two goals: Increasing penalties against unauthorized border crossers by putting far larger shares into formal removal proceedings rather than voluntarily returning them across the border, as had been longstanding practice; and making noncitizens with criminal records the top enforcement target. While there were fewer removals and returns under the Obama administration than each of the two prior administrations, those declines must be understood against the backdrop of a significant reduction in border apprehensions that resulted from a sharp decrease in unauthorized inflows, in particular of Mexicans. Analysts have attributed this trend, which began under the Bush administration, to improved economic conditions in Mexico, reduced postrecession job demand in the

"The Obama Record on Deportations: Deporter in Chief or Not?" by Muzaffar Chishti, Sarah Pierce, and Jessica Bolter, Migration Information Source (the online journal of the Migration Policy Institute), January 26, 2017, http://www.migrationpolicy.org/article /obama-record-deportations-deporter-chief-or-not. Reprinted by permission.

United States, ramped-up enforcement, and the increased use of different enforcement tactics at the border.

The enforcement priorities and policies, which evolved over the years, represented a significant departure from those of the Bush and Clinton administrations. As detailed here, the Obama-era policies represented the culmination of a gradual but consistent effort to narrow its enforcement focus to two key groups: The deportation of criminals and recent unauthorized border crossers.

The most recent enforcement figures released by the Department of Homeland Security (DHS) on December 30 offer the latest evidence of these trends. Eighty-five percent of all removals and returns during fiscal year (FY) 2016 were of noncitizens who had recently crossed the U.S. border unlawfully. Of the remainder, who were removed from the U.S. interior, more than 90 percent had been convicted of what DHS defines as serious crimes.

Border apprehensions and removals increased in FY 2016 compared to the prior year, DHS reported. In FY 2016, DHS carried out 530,250 apprehensions and 344,354 removals, compared to 462,388 apprehensions and 333,341 removals a year earlier. Despite the increase, these numbers were far lower than the peak of enforcement operations at the beginning of the Obama years, after he inherited a robust enforcement regime from his predecessors. These numbers dipped as new enforcement priorities were put in place, before rebounding slightly at the end of the Obama presidency.

Obama Inherits a Formidable Immigration Machinery

President Obama inherited a more legally robust and better-resourced immigration enforcement regime than his predecessors had. A series of laws in 1996 established new grounds for deportation, penalties for the crimes of illegal entry and re-entry, mandates for detention of deportable noncitizens, and a framework for cooperative arrangements on immigration enforcement between the federal government and state and local law enforcement agencies. Though authorized during the Clinton administration, many of these enforcement tools were not deployed and fully resourced until the Bush administration, mostly in the aftermath of the September 11, 2001 terrorist attacks.

Beginning in 2002, the federal government began 287(g) agreements, allowing state and local law enforcement officials to perform certain immigration enforcement functions. By the end of the Bush administration, more than 70 such agreements had been signed.

In 2003, Congress created DHS, including in it all immigration functions. U.S. Customs and Border Protection (CBP), the DHS component responsible for enforcement at the border, saw its border agent manpower rise from 10,000 in 2003 to 17,000 in 2008. Over the same period, U.S. Immigration and Customs Enforcement (ICE), the DHS component responsible for interior enforcement, experienced an increase in agents from 2,700 to 5,000.

At the border, CBP in 2005 introduced the Consequence Delivery System (CDS), designed to toughen the tactics used against unauthorized crossers in hopes of deterring future entry attempts. Instead of allowing unauthorized entrants to return to Mexico voluntarily, without any meaningful legal consequences, formal removal proceedings became far more common as did criminal charges for illegal entry or re-entry.

In addition, in the years following 9/11, immigration, criminal, and national-security screening systems across executive-branch agencies were expanded, upgraded, and integrated. These interoperable data systems became accessible to consular and immigration officials, as well as to local law enforcement. The Bush administration, in its final days, launched Secure Communities, a program allowing the fingerprints of those arrested by local law enforcement to be matched against federal criminal and immigration databases operated by the Federal Bureau of Investigation (FBI) and DHS.

Taken together, these combined enforcement initiatives resulted in a record high of nearly 360,000 formal removals in FY 2008—234,000 of them from the interior of the United States.

The Obama Deportation Record: A Shift from Returns to Removals

When President Obama took office in 2009, his administration abandoned some Bush-era strategies, such as worksite enforcement operations, but allowed others to scale up. By 2013, Secure Communities was operational in all jails and prisons in the United States. And the Border Patrol began systematically applying CDS border-wide starting in 2011.

Congressional funding for immigration enforcement continued to rise. In FY 2012, federal immigration enforcement funding reached nearly $18 billion—a figure 24 percent higher than funding allocated to all other principal federal criminal law enforcement agencies combined (the FBI, Drug Enforcement Administration, Secret Service, U.S. Marshals Service, and the Bureau of Alcohol, Tobacco, Firearms, and Explosives).

As a result of these resources and strategies, noncitizen removals increased significantly, while apprehensions and overall deportations both remained far lower than the numbers seen under the Bush and Clinton administrations.

These figures demonstrate the Obama administration's focus on formal removals instead of returns, with formal removals under Obama far outpacing those of the Bush and Clinton administrations even as returns were far lower. This policy to ensure that removals have a lasting legal consequence likely reduced the number of unauthorized immigrants attempting to cross the border multiple times: Overall, recidivism along the border fell from 29 percent in FY 2007 to 14 percent in FY 2014, and was much higher for migrants given voluntary return (31 percent) than for those subjected to formal removal (18 percent), according to CDS data.

Evolution of Enforcement: Prioritizing Criminals and Recent Border Crossers

Over the course of the Obama administration, there was a pronounced shift in focus to the removal of recent border crossers and criminals rather than ordinary status violators apprehended in the U.S. interior. The underlying reasoning was to deter illegal border crossing and remove unauthorized immigrants before they become integrated into U.S. communities. Interior removals decreased sharply from 181,798 in FY 2009 to 65,332 in FY 2016, while border removals stayed high and increased, from 207,525 to 279,022 over the same period.

The combined number of individuals removed and returned decreased significantly between the first and second Obama terms: from 3.2 million to 2.1 million. This decline was driven nearly entirely, as described above, by the decrease in the number of individuals voluntarily returned, rather than formally removed. From the first to second term, returns decreased significantly, from 1,609,249 to 593,104, while removals fell only slightly, from 1,575,423 to 1,518,785.

Also, removal priorities were increasingly focused on removing noncitizens convicted of crimes. In 2009, 51 percent of interior removals were of individuals convicted of what DHS described as serious crimes. In 2016, DHS reported that more than 90 percent of interior removals were of noncitizens convicted of serious crimes.

In November 2014, President Obama announced a number of further changes in immigration enforcement, including agencywide policy guidance on which categories of removable noncitizens should be the highest priority for enforcement. Three levels were detailed:

- **Priority 1:** National security threats, noncitizens apprehended immediately at the border, gang members, and noncitizens convicted of felonies or aggravated felonies as defined in immigration law.
- **Priority 2:** Noncitizens convicted of three or more misdemeanors or one serious misdemeanor, those who entered or re-entered the United States unlawfully after January 1, 2014, and those who have significantly abused visa or visa waiver programs.
- **Priority 3:** Noncitizens subject to a final order of removal issued on or after January 1, 2014.

The priorities codified a trend initiated in 2009.

Once announced in 2014, the DHS enforcement priorities became even more sharply focused on criminals and recent arrivals. In a statement, DHS reported that in FY 2015 and FY 2016, more than 99 percent of all removals and returns fell within the three priorities. In FY 2015, 92 percent of removals and returns occurred within Priority 1, a rate that rose to 94 percent in FY 2016. Some analysts attribute the sharper focus on the top priorities to the fact that the 2014 guidelines, unlike ones issued in 2010 and 2011, applied to all DHS immigration agencies, while the earlier ones were issued by and applied only to ICE.

Obama's Mixed Legacy and Looking Ahead to Enforcement under the Trump Administration

While the Obama administration record is characterized by much higher removals than preceding administrations, it also shows less focus on increasing absolute numbers of overall deportations and a higher priority on targeting the removals of recently arrived unauthorized immigrants and criminals. The administration also placed a much lower priority on removing those who had established roots in U.S. communities and had no criminal records. This prioritization was achieved by a slowly evolving but deliberate policy, highlighted by the administration's November 2014 executive actions on immigration.

The process of focusing and targeting enforcement resources has set the initial stage for the Trump administration. This week President Donald Trump signed two executive orders promising wide-ranging expansions of the enforcement system, including priorities that focus on removing not only noncitizens with criminal records, but also those who have committed potentially criminal acts or who have abused public benefits. However, like Obama, only his eventual record on immigration will tell how it compares with his predecessors' in terms of prioritizing overall numbers of removals and the categories of individuals being removed.

National Policy Beat in Brief

United States Ends "Wet-Foot, Dry-Foot" Policy on Cuban Migrants

Following months of secret negotiations, the United States and Cuba announced on January 12 that the Department of Homeland Security (DHS) has ended the "wet-foot, dry-foot" policy on Cuban migrants entering the United States. A key component of this shift involves the Cuban government's agreement to accept the return of Cuban nationals deported by the United States. The policy, established in 1995, allowed Cuban migrants who reached U.S. land to be paroled into the country, while those intercepted at sea were returned to Cuba. Under the 1996 Cuban Adjustment Act, Cuban migrants who successfully make it to the United States are able to adjust their status to that of permanent residents (i.e. green card holders) after one year. Now, Cuban migrants entering without valid visas or travel documents will be treated as any other noncitizen, including being subject to expedited removal. Those intercepted at sea will be treated as before. In addition to ending the wet-foot, dry-foot policy, the United States rescinded the Cuban Medical Professional Parole Program, which allowed Cuban medical professionals serving abroad to seek parole to enter the United States at U.S. embassies. Havana has long pressed the United States to end the medical professional parole program, as well as the wet-foot, dry-foot policy, which it claimed encourages dangerous migration journeys and human trafficking. The wet foot, dry foot announcement follows the normalization of U.S.-Cuba diplomatic relations announced in December 2014. The number of Cubans arriving in the United States has nearly doubled since fiscal year (FY) 2014, from 25,338 then to 48,520 through the first ten months of FY 2016.

Trump Nominates and Senate Confirms Marine General John Kelly as Homeland Security Secretary

President Donald Trump nominated retired Marine General John Kelly as Homeland Security Secretary. The Senate then confirmed the nomination on January 20, and he was sworn in the same day. Kelly served for 45 years in the Marines and from 2012 to 2016 headed the U.S. Southern Command, which oversees U.S. military operations in Central and South America. Kelly's confirmation hearing on January 10 focused on a variety of security- and immigration-related topics, including illegal immigration and border security. When asked about construction of further barriers at the U.S.-Mexico border, Kelly stated that a wall alone would not stem migration flows, and instead argued for "a layered approach," involving technology, personnel, and cooperation with countries south of the United States. He emphasized the importance of addressing the root causes of migration in El Salvador, Guatemala, and Honduras, including violence and lack of economic opportunity. Kelly also declined to directly address whether individuals granted Deferred Action for Childhood Arrivals (DACA) under the Obama administration would be priorities for removal, expressed doubt about the legality of so-called sanctuary city policies, and stated that he would not support vetting immigrants based solely on ethnicity or religion.

Senators Introduce Bills to Protect DACA Beneficiaries

A bipartisan group of senators has introduced a bill that would provide protections for some young people who came to the United States as children and received relief from deportation under the Deferred Action for Childhood Arrivals (DACA) program created by President Obama. Sens. Richard Durbin (D-IL) and Lindsey Graham (R-SC) introduced the Bar Removal of Individuals who Dream and Grow Our Economy (BRIDGE) Act on December 9. The bill would create a program identical to the DACA program, the 2012 Obama executive action that allows qualified unauthorized immigrants brought to the United States as children to apply for work authorization and temporary protection against removal. During the campaign, President Donald Trump committed to rescinding a number of Obama executive actions on immigration, including DACA. The BRIDGE Act would grant DACA beneficiaries and those who meet DACA eligibility requirements benefits that would be identical to those granted under DACA for three years following the date of enactment of the legislation. In addition, the bill prohibits the use of personal information submitted in DACA applications for deportation purposes, except in cases of threats to national security or a felony investigation.

Arizona Republican Sen. Jeff Flake, a cosponsor of the BRIDGE Act, also introduced the Securing Active and Fair Enforcement (SAFE) Act, which ties the protection measures proposed in the BRIDGE Act to additional enforcement measures. The SAFE Act, which includes language identical to the BRIDGE Act, would also require the Department of Homeland Security (DHS) to hold without release unauthorized immigrants convicted of or arrested for major crimes, and would require the deportation of those noncitizens within 90 days of detention. Both bills were reintroduced in the 115th Congress on January 12.

Obama Administration Dismantles NSEERS Regulations

In December the Obama administration rescinded regulations for the National Security Entry-Exit Registration System (NSEERS), a national registry program established in 2002 in the aftermath of the 9/11 terrorist attacks for visitors from countries where terrorist groups were present. The program has been dormant since 2011, but advocates pressed the president to rescind the regulations out of concern that they could be utilized by President-elect Trump once in office. Trump promised during his campaign to create a registry of Muslims in the United States, and Republicans specifically called for the renewal of NSEERS in their 2016 party platform.

Temporary Protected Status for Yemen and Somalia Extended

On January 4, Homeland Security Secretary Jeh Johnson redesignated Yemen for Temporary Protected Status (TPS) and extended the designation for an additional 18 months, due to the persistence of armed conflict and the continued deterioration of conditions for civilians in the country. Yemen was originally designated for TPS in September 2015. To be eligible, Yemeni nationals and those who last habitually resided in Yemen must have continuously resided in the United States since January 4, 2017 and have been continuously physically present since March 4, 2017. This TPS designation will last from March 4 through September 3, 2018. In addition, on January 17, Johnson extended the TPS designation for Somalia for an additional 18 months, effective March 18 through September 17, 2018. TPS grants work authorization and protection from deportation to certain nationals of designated countries deemed unsafe for repatriation due to ongoing armed conflict or the effects of a natural disaster. In total, 13 countries are currently designated for TPS: El Salvador, Guinea, Haiti, Honduras, Liberia, Nepal, Nicaragua, Sierra Leone, Somalia, Sudan, South Sudan, Syria, and Yemen.

State Policy Beat in Brief

Lawsuit on Texas Immigrant Harboring Law Heard in Federal Court

On January 5, a three-judge panel of the Fifth U.S. Circuit Court of Appeals heard arguments over the implementation of a provision of a 2015 Texas border security bill that makes it a crime to conceal or harbor unauthorized migrants. The Mexican American Legal Defense and Educational Fund (MALDEF) first challenged the harboring provision in January 2016, arguing it violates the supremacy clause of the U.S. Constitution, which gives the federal government exclusive authority over immigration enforcement. In April, a federal judge blocked enforcement of the harboring provision while the case was ongoing. The plaintiffs, two landlords who do not inquire about the immigration status of tenants and the head of an immigrant-service organization, contend that under the harboring provision, they could be accused of a crime for continuing to house unauthorized immigrants. The Texas Attorney General's office argues this concern is unwarranted because the bill did not include a specific punishment for renting to or sheltering unauthorized immigrants.

Court Rules DACA Recipients in Georgia
Eligible for In-State Tuition

A Superior Court judge in suburban Atlanta ruled on December 30 that DACA beneficiaries are eligible for in-state tuition rates at Georgia universities. A 2008 state law provides that individuals who are "legally in this state" are eligible for in-state tuition, a rate that is one-third of out-of-state tuition. The ten plaintiffs, all DACA recipients, successfully argued that they qualified for in-state tuition under the 2008 law due to their federally established legal presence. The Georgia Board of Regents appealed the decision, and although the Fulton County judge, Gail Tusan, refused to put her order on hold during the process, the Board of Regents has also asked the Court of Appeals to put it on hold. As of January 11, the Court of Appeals had not made public any decision on whether it will allow the judge's order to go into effect during the appeals process.

Mexico Assumes Bulk of Southern US Immigration Enforcement

Genevieve Leigh and Toby Reese

Genevieve Leigh and Toby Reese are frequent contributors to the World Socialist Web Site.

Over the past six years the United States and Mexican governments have collectively apprehended nearly 1 million refugees fleeing to the United States from the Northern Triangle countries—El Salvador, Guatemala and Honduras—deporting more than 800,000, including more than 40,000 children. Nearly 10 percent of the Northern Triangle countries' total population have reportedly left the region.

The unceasing flow of refugees has compelled the political establishment to take a series of measures in an attempt to contain the crisis. More recently, the strategy of the Obama administration has been to shift the dirty work of apprehensions and deportations to its southern neighbor, Mexico.

Under heavy pressure from Washington, Mexico implemented Programa Frontera Sur in July 2014. The plan, likely crafted by officials within the Obama administration itself, means that those refugees who previously would have reached the US border are now being intercepted by Mexican authorities.

Under the Programa Frontera Sur, Mexico has relocated over 300 immigration agents to its southern border with Guatemala to carry out the ruthless dictates of Washington. The program has included setting up mobile checkpoints and conducting regular raids on trains and migrant hostels. The Obama administration has directly supported this campaign with training, technology and intelligence. For migrants, the consequences have been devastating.

"Deporter-in-Chief: The Legacy of Obama," by Genevieve Leigh and Toby Reese, World Socialist Web Site, November 8, 2016. Reprinted by permission.

A year after its implementation in July 2014, apprehensions by the Mexican government increased by 71 percent over the same period the previous year. Likewise, apprehensions of Central Americans by the US border patrol decreased. This shift created the illusion of some measure of effective immigration reform in the US. In reality, even more migrants are being deported than previously; the only change has been in the location of apprehension. Furthermore, due to the absence or deliberate disregard of laws of due process and humanitarian norms, the migrants are often no longer even considered for temporary visas. Instead, they are forced to return, in massive numbers, to some of the most violent and desperate social conditions on the planet.

The program has taken a particularly aggressive approach to operations aimed at preventing migrants from riding north on cargo trains, known collectively as La Bestia. Migration authorities have blocked migrants from boarding trains, forcibly removed migrants from trains mid-ride, and raided establishments that migrants are known to frequent, detaining thousands in the process. There have been many reports of excessive use of force and other abuses by the authorities, including a recent shooting of a 15-year-old boy traveling from Guatemala.

The government has denied all of the charges. No longer able to board the train in Chiapas, migrants, because of the disruption of the usual route, are forced to rely on different and dangerous modes of transportation, often traveling incredible distances by foot. Without access to the networks of resources and shelters long established on the previous train route, migrants suffer immensely from vulnerabilities on their new path.

The Mexican government has turned these methods of repression, forged initially to be used against migrants, towards its own population. Earlier this year the *Guardian* found that an increasing number of indigenous Mexicans had been detained for possible deportation in Chiapas for not having a valid identification—despite the Mexican Constitution stating that individuals are able to move freely throughout the country "without necessity of a letter of security, passport, safe-conduct or any other similar requirement." It is quite common for babies who are born in indigenous communities in Chiapas, Guerrero, and Oaxaca to be born without a record of birth. Some reports estimate that as many as 7 million Mexicans do not have a registered name, identity, or nationality. Earlier this year, the WSWS learned of a woman who gave birth to a child in Chiapas and then, en route to the US, became entangled in an immigration web in which the baby became stranded without citizenship in either country.

As the tenure of the 44th United States president comes to a close, a balance sheet of the administration's "accomplishments" regarding immigration should be drawn. Despite grand promises of immigration reform in his first 100 days of office, the Obama administration proceeded to enact draconian immigration legislation and speed up deportations. Obama's actions become all the more significant when one considers that these policies were carried out while the Democratic Party, which continues to posture as a defender of working people and the poor, gained a majority in both houses of Congress after the 2008 elections.

In immigrant communities, Obama has become infamously known as "deporter-in-chief." Since 2008 there have been over 2.5 million deportations, an average of more than 1,000 per day. This is roughly double the rate that occurred under Republican president George Bush, and totals more than under any other president in US history. In 2013, there were 435,498 removals, an all-time high for a single year. In addition, the administration has prioritized using a more formal removal process, which carries greater consequences if re-entry is attempted by the immigrant. Considering that the most recent statistics only include deportations that have taken place through October 2014, it is quite possible that over 3 million immigrants have been deported to date.

After coming to office, Obama vastly expanded a program begun under Bush called Secure Communities. The program united federal, state, and local law enforcement agencies with the US Immigration and Customs Enforcement (ICE) in an effort to deport immigrants who were already living in communities, as opposed to those attempting to cross the border. A political scientist at the University of Iowa, Rene Rocha, recently told the *Christian Science Monitor*, "Prior to the Obama administration, there was very little interior enforcement, it was almost all near the border. By the end of 2011, arrests near the border and interior were equal."

The program faced extensive criticism for ripping up communities and the lack of regulation of the program's implementation. A study by UC Berkeley found that only 52 percent of individuals arrested through the program were slated to have a hearing before an immigration judge and that 39 percent of individuals arrested had a spouse or children who were US citizens, causing an impact on 88,000 families that included US citizens.

In many cases, immigrants who have temporary legal status through programs such as Deferred Action for Childhood Arrivals (DACA) are held in poorly regulated detention centers throughout the country with few rights. Although these individuals have received temporary legal immunity from deportation, in many states they are not eligible for Medicaid programs, nor are they eligible for the tax subsidies of the Affordable Care Act. In select states that have provided a state-funded waiver to assist the poorest sections of immigrants, such as California with Medicaid, this vulnerable section of the population is often scapegoated by the right wing for their "abuse of social programs," in a further effort to divide the working class.

The administration's "reform" measures did not only focus on immigrants already residing in the country but have also focused on strengthening Fortress America at the border. In 2010, Obama signed into legislation a bill that granted $600 million to further militarize the US-Mexico border through the buildup of thousands of border agents and the use of Predator drones to patrol from the sky.

The most recent manifestation of Obama "reform" came in September when his administration announced that it would begin the forced removal of Haitian refugees, an act only briefly postponed in the wake of Hurricane Matthew and the massing of thousands of Haitian immigrants at the US border in cities such as Tijuana, Mexico. Many of these immigrants, who fled Haiti to Brazil following the 2010 earthquake, are now being forced out of economic necessity to make the dangerous journey north from Brazil to the United States. Much like the migrants fleeing the war-torn Northern Triangle region, the Haitian migrants have now become double victims of US imperialism: first, from the devastating situation they faced in their home countries brought on by US imperialism, and later during their perilous journey in search of livable conditions.

The criminal immigration policies of the Obama administration carried out over the last eight years are yet another indictment of the increasingly Orwellian nature of the US political establishment. The great "anti-war" candidate became the first president in history to keep the US at war throughout two full terms in office. Universal health care has turned out to be nothing short of a restructuring of the system to benefit big business. The alleged candidate of working people has overseen the largest transfer of wealth to the top 1 percent in history. As his presidency comes to a close, we should add to the balance sheet immigration "reform" that has turned out to mean the ruthless deportation of more immigrants than any other administration in US history.

For all intents and purposes, Hillary Clinton can be expected to continue the same harsh policies as the Obama administration if she is voted into the White House on November 8. While Clinton demagogically harangues Donald Trump for his plans to build more walls, she has been a firm supporter of deportations, and voted for the increased securing of the border through building a 700-mile barrier between the US and Mexico in the Secure Fence Act of 2006 (a bill also approved by Obama as a senator). Clinton is on record in January of this year trying to distance herself from Trump by dishonestly quibbling over semantics and stating that she supported the building of a "fence" and not a "wall." Based on the Obama experience, it should be clear that whatever rhetoric is decided upon, the reality will be increased attacks on defenseless migrants.

Most Deportees Under Obama Committed Only Minor Infractions

America's Voice

The mission of America's Voice (AV) and the America's Voice Education Fund (AVEF) is to harness the power of American voices and American values to enact policy change that guarantees full labor, civil, and political rights for immigrants and their families.

I n a conference call today with reporters, immigration experts and community leaders reacted to the latest reports about who the Department of Homeland Security (DHS) is actually deporting, and how many could actually be considered high-priority offenders under a common-sense definition, rather than Moms and Dads trying to care for their families.

Comprehensive data and analysis from the *New York Times* and Transactional Access Records Clearinghouse (TRAC) show that despite Obama Administration claims that they are focusing deportations on "convicted criminals," most individuals who are deported have only traffic or immigration violations, or no offense at all.

According to the *New York Times*, nearly 2/3 of the 2 million deportations carried out by the Obama Administration were of "people who had committed minor infractions, including traffic violations, or had no criminal record at all. Twenty percent—or about 394,000—of the cases involved people convicted of serious crimes, including drug-related offenses, the records show." A new report from TRAC shows a similar trend. For Fiscal Year 2013, for example, 42% of deportees had no convictions whatsoever. Twenty-seven percent had been convicted of a traffic or immigration offense and only 12% met the government's highest priority (Level 1 crimes).

"Who Is the Obama Administration Really Deporting?," AV Press Releases, America's Voice, April 8, 2014. Reprinted by permission.

According to Lynn Tramonte, Deputy Director of America's Voice:

> According to TRAC, if you define "convicted criminal" the way the Administration does, and include people guilty of traffic offenses, most Americans would be criminals. And, if you follow the DHS definition of a "border resident," which includes anyone living within 100 miles of an international border, most Americans would qualify according to the ACLU. Despite the Obama Administration's insistence otherwise, the vast majority of people they are deporting are ordinary folks with families, jobs, and lives in the United States. The Times and TRAC are exposing the facts.

In fact, under the Obama Administration, "there has been an absolute decline in the number of noncitizens removed who have been convicted of any crime apart from traffic and immigration" according to TRAC. "During FY 2010 these individuals numbered 116,884. By FY 2013 they had declined to only 103,676. This means that the trumpeted increase in the number of 'convicted criminals' ICE has deported resulted entirely from jacking up the deportation of noncitizens whose most serious criminal conviction was a traffic or an immigration offense," the report explains.

TRAC data also presents a searing indictment of the Secure Communities program, which involves state and local police in immigration enforcement. They provide just the latest round of evidence to show that, despite the fact that this program is supposed to be going after serious criminals, it has actually triggered deportation of millions of immigrants who do not meet that definition in any way. And despite claims that the program would be "blind" to race and ethnicity, in fact it has been used by police officers and local sheriffs to go on fishing expeditions for immigrants. As the data shows, the U.S. Border Patrol and ICE appear all too willing to comply.

During the call, Veronica Dahlberg, Executive Director of HOLA Ohio and Monica García, Regional Coordinator of the Border Network for Human Rights in Las Cruces, New Mexico, talked about trends in their own border communities—Veronica in northeast Ohio along the Lake Erie border with Canada, and Monica in New Mexico.

"In this quiet, small town in Ohio, families who have carved out a little piece of the American Dream, are getting ripped apart. The *New York Times* article finally is shedding light on what is really happening versus what the administration's message of what is happening," said Dahlberg. "We have a very strong Border Patrol presence here in Ohio and they have created relationships with all of the police departments in these small towns and have said, 'if you see anybody who looks suspicious, call us.' This is what we are living now—very heavy handed enforcement that's part of everyday life now. What we really want is for the Administration to change their own policies that are truly hurting families in our community."

Added Monica García, Regional Coordinator at the Border Network for Human Rights in Las Cruces, New Mexico:

> *Most of the deportations in our records, they're not criminals. They're people who work, they've lived here for many years, their record is clean, and they're being deported. The Border Patrol doesn't know what kind of people they're taking out of our communities. They need to know who they're deporting.*

David Leopold, Immigration Attorney, Cleveland, OH, and Past President of American Immigration Lawyers Association, explained some of the legal aspects of the government's deportation decisions and classifications. In particular, he pointed to the Department of Justice's role in actually prosecuting immigrants for immigration-related offenses, so that they end up with a criminal record and months or years in jail before eventually being deported.

The *New York Times* digs into the Obama administration's decision to charge immigration violators who previously would have been removed without formal charges:

> *In the final year of the Bush administration, more than a quarter of those caught in the United States with no criminal record were returned to their native countries without charges. In 2013, charges were filed in more than 90 percent of those types of cases, which*

prohibit immigrants from returning for at least five years and exposing those caught returning illegally to prison time.

And according to TRAC, the number of individuals deported after being prosecuted for an immigration violation has risen 167% under Obama. Tramonte said:

This is a policy decision at the Department of Justice (DOJ) to go the extra mile and turn ordinary immigrants into federal criminals before they are deported. So far, most of the attention on the need for reforms has focused on Jeh Johnson and the DHS. Attorney General Eric Holder and the DOJ need to be included.

As Leopold concluded:

You've had 3-4 major reports in the last few weeks, from the Pew Report to the Immigration Policy Center to the New York Times report this weekend to the TRAC report today, which all find that contrary to what the Administration says, the people who are being removed have equity and don't deserve to be deported. It's mind-boggling that we're removing parents of US citizens essentially for being bad drivers. Most Americans would qualify as criminals when it comes to ICE. The Administration needs to better protect these people who are being deported.

Obama Administration Immigration Policy Draws Responses from Both Sides

Marcus Stern

Marcus Stern served as a reporter at ProPublica and also worked for Copley News Service in Washington, DC.

The Obama administration has changed the nation's immigration enforcement strategy in ways that will reduce the threat of deportation for millions of undocumented immigrants and will likely blunt the impact of any state laws designed to deport vast numbers of people.

The changes are the little-discussed byproducts of the administration's well-publicized decision to focus its deportation efforts on immigrants who have committed serious crimes.

To remove the "worst of the worst," the administration reasons, it can't allow the nation's immigration courts and detention centers to remain clogged with generally law-abiding immigrants who have lived in the country for a long time and probably would be legalized under comprehensive immigration reform legislation.

The administration's strategy has been revealed in recent months through internal memos, testimony and new guidelines that direct deportation officers to generally refrain from deporting certain groups of immigrants.

- In a June 30 memo, John Morton, director of Immigration and Customs Enforcement (ICE), stressed the new priorities to his officers around the country: Use the agency's limited resources to find and deport immigrants who have committed serious crimes rather than scoop up longtime undocumented immigrants who haven't.
- On July 1, ICE's executive associate director of management,

Daniel Ragsdale, testified in the administration's lawsuit against Arizona's immigration law that ICE officers have been told to "exercise discretion" when deciding whether to detain "long-time lawful permanent residents, juveniles, the immediate family members of U.S. citizens, veterans, members of the armed forces and their families, and others with illnesses or special circumstances."

- An internal memo leaked to the media in July discussed ways the administration could adjust existing regulations so certain groups, such as college students and the spouses of military personnel, could legalize their status or at least avoid deportation if Congress doesn't pass comprehensive immigration reform.
- The memo came from ICE's sister agency, U.S. Citizens and Immigration Service (USCIS), which rules on applications for visas, work permits and citizenship. USCIS played down the draft as a brainstorming device. Nonetheless, it underscored the administration's view that legalization was more appropriate than deportation for many people.
- On Aug. 20, Morton ordered ICE officials to begin dismissing deportation cases against people who have credible immigration applications pending and haven't committed serious crimes. According to the *Houston Chronicle*, immigration attorneys who went to court last month anticipating their clients' deportations were stunned to learn that many of the cases had been dismissed.
- Perhaps the most dramatic shift in enforcement strategy was outlined in a draft proposed directive from Morton, posted last month on ICE's website for public comment. It would prohibit police from using misdemeanor traffic stops to flag people to ICE for deportation, even though traffic stops have been credited with increasing the number of deportations in recent years. Some exceptions would be made, including for immigrants with serious criminal records.

The president doesn't need congressional approval to make any of these changes because the executive branch has wide leeway in how it administers the laws Congress writes.

But the administration's new direction puts it on a collision course with those who believe the nation's immigration laws should be strictly enforced and that all illegal immigrants should be deported.

Rep. Steve King, R-Iowa, the top Republican on the House immigration subcommittee, said that by making exceptions, ICE is "thumbing its nose at the law." And the union representing ICE's 7,000 enforcement officers has issued a unanimous no-confidence vote that singled out Morton and an assistant, saying their new detention and removal policies were "misguided and reckless initiatives, which could ultimately put many Americans at risk."

"Everything is being driven away from arresting people just for being here illegally or low-level criminals," said a supervisory ICE agent who asked not to be identified for fear of reprisals from his superiors. "They're using 'cost savings' and the 'worst of the worst' as their justification. But to me and those inside, it's all politics. They want us to stay away from the illegals who are living and working here and not committing serious crimes until such time as they can get immigration reform passed."

The changes have also drawn complaints from immigration advocates, who say deportations under Obama have reached record highs and that the immigrants who remain behind are still living in limbo, without work permits, Social Security cards or driver's licenses.

"This isn't a free ticket," said Raed Gonzalez, one of the Houston-area attorneys whose clients' cases were dropped last month. "This is termination without prejudice, which means that the government can put them back into proceedings at any time."

People close to the administration acknowledge that the new strategy doesn't please activists on either side of the immigration debate. But they say it's the best Obama can do without immigration reform legislation from Congress.

In an interview with ProPublica, Morton, the ICE director, said the administration's strategy will lead to smarter enforcement, not softer enforcement. Given that there are now more than 10 million people in the country illegally and that a record amount of money is being spent on immigration enforcement in an era of unprecedented budget deficits, he said it makes sense to target people who pose the biggest threat to public safety or national security.

"Congress provides enough money to deport a little less than 400,000 people and in an era of limited resources, who should those 400,000 be?" Morton said. "My perspective is those 400,000 people shouldn't be the first 400,000 people in the door but rather 400,000 people who reflect some considered government enforcement policy based on a rational set of objectives and priorities.

Deportations have increased dramatically in recent years, from 189,000 in 2001 to 387,000 in 2009. Much of that increase has been accomplished by doing what the administration is now trying to avoid: deporting large numbers of people who haven't committed serious crimes.

This year, however, that trend has taken a sharp turn, according to a report released in July by TRAC, a Syracuse University program that gathers and analyzes government data. While more than half of the people being held for deportation haven't committed crimes, the percentage of those who have rose from 27 percent to 43 percent this year.

The number of criminal immigrants removed by ICE "has already broken all previous records, and climbed to an all-time high," according to the report. "The removal pace of criminal aliens in FY 2010 is fully 60 percent higher than in the last year of the Bush administration, and at least a third (37%) higher than in the first year of the Obama administration."

The administration's new strategy—including many of its key points and phrases—echoes a February 2009 report (PDF) by the Migration Policy Institute, a nonprofit research center, which produced it in hopes that the administration might use it as a blueprint for its enforcement strategy.

"What they've done is what any good law enforcement agency does," said Donald Kerwin, who co-authored the 2009 report with Doris Meissner, head of the Immigration and Naturalization

Service under President Bill Clinton. "They can always jack up the numbers but does it have any impact? And the answer is no, it doesn't."

Trying to Unclog the Immigration Courts

Deportations have doubled in the past decade in part because Congress has steadily increased the removals budget, from $1.2 billion to $2.5 billion in the last five years alone. But the numbers also have been boosted by two ICE programs—287(g) and Secure Communities—which use local police to help identify and detain more undocumented immigrants than ICE agents could ever pick up by themselves. Twenty-two states are now considering laws that would require their police to become involved in immigration enforcement.

The two programs have been so successful that the nation's immigration courts had a record backlog of 248,000 cases earlier this year, according to another TRAC report. Immigrants now wait an average of 459 days for their cases to be heard, with the average rising to 643 days in California. Most of the immigrants are released pending their hearings—including some who are a threat to public safety—because it is too costly for the government to hold them for such long periods.

The 287(g) program, named for the section of the immigration law that created it, permits state and local police, with training and supervision from ICE, to access ICE databases and decide whether someone they've stopped or taken to jail on other charges should be referred to ICE for deportation.

Seventy-one jurisdictions in 26 states now have 287(g) agreements with ICE, and about 40 more are pending, according to ICE spokesman Richard Rocha. Although the program was enacted in 1996, the agreements didn't come until 2002 and only in the last three years has the program begun to spread.

Authorities in jurisdictions that use 287(g) praise its effectiveness.

"We've seen a lot of success with it," said Stacey Bourbonnais, a spokeswoman for the Gwinnet County, Ga., Sheriff's Department. During the first half of this fiscal year, Gwinnet County helped

ICE put 1,500 immigrants into deportation proceedings.

But immigrant rights groups complain that 287(g) encourages ethnic profiling and targets people who have committed traffic violations and other minor crimes. Last year, ICE responded to those complaints by rewriting the 287(g) agreements to specify that the program is intended to target criminal undocumented immigrants. But complaints have persisted and the Department of Homeland Secuirty, ICE's parent agency, is now reviewing the program.

An official familiar with the ongoing review predicted it will lead the administration to shut down the program. If it does, it would be a victory for immigrant rights groups and a blow to state and local enforcement agencies that have chosen to participate.

The second program, Secure Communities, operates in 17,553 jurisdictions in 23 states, and ICE hopes to make it available to jurisdictions nationwide by 2013. Like 287(g), it allows local officers to tap into ICE databases. But the local police and ICE agents play no role in deciding who should be put into the deportation pipeline.

The administration says that focusing on "the worst of the worst" is vital to ICE's primary mission of national security and public safety and can work only if the pipeline out of the country isn't clogged, as it is now, with people who aren't a significant danger.

But King, the Iowa Republican, says the Obama administration had another choice when it came to unclogging the system: It "should have come to Congress and asked for more judges, more prison beds and more prosecutors" so the courts could quickly process all the undocumented immigrants they received. The goal, King said, is to remove everybody deportable under the law.

Some experts say that deporting 10 million people living in the United States illegally, if that were possible at all, would take 20 years and more than $50 billion in taxpayer money. But King is undaunted.

"If that were the formula that got us to the point where we'd reestablished the rule of law, I would support that," he said. "I think that's going to be about $8 (annually) a person for every American. I think that's a pretty cheap price to pay to reestablish the rule of law."

A Closer Look at Obama's Immigration Policy

Scott Horsley

Scott Horsley is a White House correspondent for NPR News, reporting on the policy and politics of the Trump administration. He took up the White House beat in 2009 after serving as a San Diego-based business correspondent.

I n a speech Wednesday night, Donald Trump will lay out—and clarify—his proposed immigration policy.

His stance on immigration has appeared to change more in the past 10 days than it has in the past 10 months.

But perhaps the most unexpected element of the recent shifts in rhetoric is that Trump has praised President Obama's work on immigration enforcement, a surprising turn for a Republican candidate.

"What people don't know is that Obama got tremendous numbers of people out of the country. Bush, the same thing. Lots of people were brought out of the country with the existing laws. Well, I'm going to do the same thing," Trump said last week to Fox News' Bill O'Reilly.

That's true, to an extent. Ahead of Trump's speech, here are five things to know about how President Obama has enforced immigration laws over the past eight years.

Deportations Increased Under President Obama, At First

Deportations, or "removals" as the Department of Homeland Security calls them, increased in each of the first four years President Obama was in office, topping 400,000 in fiscal year 2012. Obama oversaw more deportations than George W. Bush did, just as Bush oversaw more than Bill Clinton did. The trend toward increased deportations began with the 1996 passage of the Illegal Immigration Reform and Immigrant Responsibility Act and accelerated after the Sept. 11 attacks, with growing budgets for the DHS agencies that enforce immigration law. Formal removal has largely replaced informal "return" for those caught in the country illegally. Removal carries stiffer consequences and it's increasingly carried out without judicial review.

Deportations Have Dipped in the Past Three Years

Deportations peaked in fiscal year 2012, and have declined in each of the three years since then, dropping to 235,413 in fiscal year 2015. The decline in deportations mirrors a drop in apprehensions along the southwest border with Mexico. According to U.S. Customs and Border Protection, apprehensions so far this year are running slightly ahead of 2015, but well below the pace of the two previous years. In addition, deportations from the interior of the United States have been dropping steadily since the first year of the Obama administration.

Odds of Deportation Depend a Lot on Geography and Timing

President Obama's approach to immigration enforcement is really two very different approaches: one for those caught near the border, the other for immigrants found living illegally in the interior. How long an immigrant has been here makes a difference as well. Like others before it, the Obama administration says it doesn't have the resources or the desire to deport millions of immigrants whose only crime was entering the country illegally. So, it has focused its enforcement efforts on particular targets: namely those caught near the border, those who've committed crimes and those who appear to have arrived in 2014 or later.

"The result is sharply different enforcement pictures at the border and within the United States," according to a report from the nonpartisan Migration Policy Institute. "At the border, there is a near zero tolerance system, where unauthorized immigrants are increasingly subject to formal removal and criminal charges. Within the country, there is greater flexibility."

In the last year of the Bush administration, 64 percent of deportations were from the interior of the country. By last year, interior deportations had shrunk to less than 30 percent of the total. While the Obama administration has focused enforcement efforts along the border, not everyone apprehended there is a new, first-time arrival. Some may have longstanding ties and family members elsewhere in the U.S.

The administration stresses that a growing proportion of those who are deported have criminal records: 59 percent last year, up from 31 percent in fiscal year 2008.

Illegal Immigration from Mexico Has Dropped in Recent Years, but Many from Central America Still Attempt to Cross

Border Patrol apprehensions, which the government sees as a barometer of illegal border-crossing attempts, have been dropping for the past decade and a half. The Border Patrol apprehended 337,117 people nationwide in fiscal year 2015. That's down nearly 30 percent from the previous year and nearly 80 percent below the peak in 2000. Monthly figures through July of this year show a slight uptick, but apprehensions are still well below 2014 levels.

Late last year, the Pew Research Center reported that in the previous five years, more Mexicans had left the United States than entered. The center suggested tough border enforcement and a slow-growing U.S. economy contributed to reversing what had been "one of the largest mass migrations in modern history."

While the influx of border-crossers from Mexico may have slowed or stopped, the U.S. continues to attract a sizable number of immigrants from Central America. Officers patrolling the southwest border of the United States apprehended 172,165 immigrants from countries other than Mexico during the first 10 months of the fiscal year.

The Administration Has Used Its Discretion to Shape Immigration Enforcement, Except When the Federal Courts Said No

In 2012, the administration granted a temporary reprieve from deportation to certain immigrants who were brought to this country illegally as children. More than 600,000 young people took advantage of the offer, which also enabled them to obtain work permits.

In late 2014, President Obama tried to expand that reprieve to several million immigrants who are the parents of U.S. citizens or green card holders. Texas and other states challenged the move in federal court, and it remains on hold after a short-handed U.S. Supreme Court was unable to reach a decision this year.

Obama Pushed for Immigration Reform While Deporting Millions

Alex Nowrasteh

Alex Nowrasteh is an analyst of immigration policy currently working at the Center for Global Liberty and Prosperity of the Cato Institute, a libertarian think tank located in Washington, DC.

President Obama has a mixed record on immigration. On one hand, he is the most stringent enforcer of immigration laws in American history—far outstripping the deportation numbers of the George W. Bush and earlier administrations. On the other hand, his executive actions have helped shield large swaths of illegal immigrants from deportation.

The Obama administration has deported 2.5 million illegal immigrants. This record-setting pace of deportations holds up even when counting only those from the interior of the United States—1.18 million of them under Obama's watch. By contrast, the Bush administration deported 2 million people and a confirmed 555,164 from the interior of the United States. Interior deportation numbers for the first two years of the Bush administration aren't available but under any realistic assumption his numbers could not possibly exceed Obama's.

The chance that an illegal immigrant will be deported under the Obama administration is an average of 1.48 a year compared to 0.83 percent under the Bush administration. The Obama administration has surged enforcement immigration laws against employers—issuing 15.5 times as many fines against employers and 8.3 times as many arrests for violating immigration laws as his predecessor. Detention for those who crossed the border has also increased under the Obama administration—including for many of the roughly 227,000 children and families who have surged across the border since 2010.

And this is all on the heels of expanding a small Bush-era interior enforcement program called Secure Communities (S-COMM) from just a handful of jurisdictions to virtually the entire country. S-COMM forced local police departments to cooperate with the federal government in removing illegal immigrants they arrested. S-COMM's purpose was to remove dangerous criminals but it had zero effect on actual crime rates according to research published in the prestigious *Journal of Law and Economics* and the journal *Criminology and Public Policy.* In 2015, the Obama administration replaced S-COMM with a more targeted program whereby the government primarily goes after serious offenders.

There is just no two ways about it, President Obama initiated and expanded a harsher immigration enforcement regime than President Bush or any other President in American history.

There is, however, another side to that story. President Obama issued a de facto temporary legalization of some illegal immigrants who were brought here as children. His first Deferred Action for Childhood Arrival (DACA) has the potential to shield about 1.7 million illegal immigrants from deportation although substantially fewer have applied for that protection. His expanded 2014 DACA announcement combined with Deferred Action for Parents of Americans has the potential to shield many more although the courts have held up its implementation due to serious Constitutional questions.

On the legal immigration front, President Obama's administration first promulgated rules to increase the cost for temporary guest worker, guaranteeing increased demand for illegal workers to fill those gaps. However, in recent years agencies under his watch have slightly liberalized rules that allow skilled workers and their families to more easily seek and gain employment in the United States.

Throughout this time, the number of illegal immigrants has held steady. In 2014 the number of illegal immigrants was 11.3 million according to the Pew Research Center—the same number as were estimated to be here when he took office. By contrast, the population of illegal immigrants grew by almost two million under the Bush administration following rapid growth in every previous administration going back to Johnson. The collapse in illegal immigrants entering the United States explains much of the stabilization but perhaps President Obama doesn't deserve any credit for that.

Douglas Massey of Princeton University attributes roughly zero credit to changing immigration enforcement. He claims that more border security actually "locked in" illegal immigrants by restricting their cross-border movement. Since the workers could not move back and forth due to the new border patrol, they sent for their families to come north. Massey estimates that there would be 5.3 million fewer illegal immigrants in the United States if immigration enforcement had not expanded since 1986.

In contrast, a report published by the Council on Foreign Relations claims that about a third of the decrease in illegal immigrants coming across the border can be explained by increased enforcement. The rest is explained by changing economic conditions, namely that the Mexican economy has improved relative to the U.S. economy. Immigration enforcement may be up but it has not affected the flow or population of illegal immigrants as much as other factors like the economy or demographics.

President Obama has a mixed immigration legacy. His executive actions have shielded hundreds of thousands from deportation and have the potential to do much more. On the other hand, he was a stringent enforcer of immigration laws and expanded their reach. President Obama did not enforce immigration perfectly—he just did so far more thoroughly than any other administration in U.S. history.

The lesson of this mixed legacy is that immigration enforcement cannot solve the illegal immigration problem and executive actions to legalize them are just a temporary and partial solution. Only Congress can put forth serious and permanent immigration reform that expands legal immigration and legalizes the current illegal immigrant population as a lasting solution to the current broken system.

CHAPTER 3

Can Deportation in the Age of Trump Be a Boon to America?

Overview: Squaring Trump's Executive Orders on Immigration with the Facts

Fiona Adamson

Fiona Adamson is a senior lecturer and associate professor in international relations at the University of London. Her research interests include transnational identity politics, international peace and security, and migration and diaspora.

The first week of the new Trump administration was a turbulent one, marked by a flurry of Presidential Executive Orders, Memoranda and Proclamations. Three of the Executive Orders focused on issues of migration and security, and have attracted much media coverage as well as widespread protests. On Wednesday January 25th President Trump signed the Executive Order on Border Security and Immigration Enforcement Improvement and the Executive Order on Enhancing Public Safety in the Interior of the United States. On Friday January 27th, he signed the Executive Order on Protecting the Nation From Terrorist Attacks by Foreign Nationals.

The first two Executive Orders lay out a range of provisions including the construction of a wall on the southern border of the United States; the expansion of detention facilities for undocumented migrants; accelerated processes of apprehension and removal for irregular migrants; and pressure on so-called "sanctuary cities." They also include a number of provisions that strip non-citizens of privacy rights, set up a new "Office for Victims of Crimes Committed by Removable Aliens," compel local officials and agencies to act as federal immigration officials, and require government agencies to publish weekly reports of crimes committed

"Trump's Executive Orders on Migration and Security: Policy Incompetence, Political Theater or Ideological Pivot?," by Fiona Adamson, senior lecturer in international relations, SOAS University of London, the Center for Migration Studies of New York (CMS), February 9, 2017. https://doi.org/10.14240/cmsesy020917. Reprinted by permission.

by non-citizens. The Executive Order on Terrorism—which received far-reaching and global attention—included a suspension for 120 days of the US Refugee Admissions Program (USRAP); a halt to the settlement of refugees from Syria; the use of religious criteria for vetting and refugee admissions; and a 90 day ban on entry to citizens from seven Muslim-majority countries—Iraq, Iran, Libya, Somalia, Sudan, Syria, and Yemen—which originally applied to dual citizens and legal permanent residents (green card holders)—a provision that was later walked back.

Taken together, the Executive Orders contain sweeping proposals that cover a range of issues relating to migration and security. Much has already been written about the detrimental effects of these Executive Orders on individuals, local communities and vulnerable populations in the United States, the multiple legal and bureaucratic obstacles they face in being implemented, and their potentially negative effects on the US economy, national security and international reputation. The Executive Order halting refugee resettlement and banning entry into the United States has also set off alarm bells as it indicates the new administration's willingness to introduce religious biases into entry, migration and refugee resettlement decisions.

The Executive Orders have been pitched by the administration as fulfilling Trump's campaign promise of "making America safe again" and significant portions of the US electorate will see them in this light. Trump received the highest levels of support from those who viewed immigration and terrorism to be the most important issues facing the country and many of his supporters have viewed the Executive Orders in a positive light and as an indication of Trump making good on his campaign promises. Indeed, more Americans appear to support the entry ban than oppose it, with 82% of Republicans registering support.

The Trump campaign spent months promoting a message that the United States was weak on migration, border control and security. He returned to this theme in his inaugural speech and it has carried forward into the new administration. For example, the Department of Homeland Security (DHS) response to the legal challenges against the Executive Order defended them as "re-establishing control over America's borders and national security." When the administration took the worrisome step of firing the acting Attorney General, Sally Yates, for calling into question the legal basis of the Executive Orders, it issued a statement calling her "weak on borders and very weak on illegal immigration" saying "it is time to get serious about protecting our country." This language suggests that the Executive Orders are designed as needed policy responses to an existing problem. This simply does not fit the facts on the ground, however, and suggests that the Executive Orders are not primarily about addressing a policy gap, but have broader political motives.

Executive Orders as Policy

The Executive Orders will be perceived by many members of the public as a policy response designed to address an existing problem. Most Americans do not have the time to study the complexities of existing migration policy and will thus rely on media sources to form their views. Many will see the Executive Orders as faithfully introducing new policies designed to "make America safe again."

If the Executive Orders are taken at face value, however, what strikes one immediately is their lack of understanding of existing United States policy on migration, border control and refugee admissions. The Executive Order on Border Security, for example, begins by claiming that there has been a "surge of illegal immigration at the southern border with Mexico." However, there has actually been a steady decrease in irregular migration from Mexico over the past fifteen years, due to a combination of enhanced border control and improvements in the Mexican economy. Similarly, the Executive Order calls for an immediate construction of a physical barrier on the US-Mexican border, yet makes no mention of the fact that there is already a fence along the US southern border that is hundreds of miles long, covering high-density areas of the border. Building a wall would thus involve spending billions of dollars on areas of the border that are in fact highly inaccessible and dangerous to cross, bringing no clear immigration control benefit. The Executive Order on Border Control also calls for hiring 5,000 new Border Control Officers. Yet a November 2016 Cato Institute Report found that there is currently a *surplus* of Border Control Agents, concluding that many of them "have little to do."

The Executive Orders also propose costly measures to increase immigration enforcement, detention and deportation. This suggests that the drafters of the Executive Orders are unaware that the number of undocumented migrants in the US is not on the rise, but has actually decreased under Obama. The Executive Orders also suggest that crime by undocumented migrants is a problem in sanctuary cities, yet research shows that crime rates are actually lower in "sanctuaries" than in non-sanctuary areas. Sanctuary counties also have higher incomes, less poverty, less reliance on public assistance and lower unemployment than non-sanctuary counties. It is no wonder that major city police chiefs have criticized and opposed the Executive Orders, citing them as detrimental to law enforcement because they erode trust between police and local communities.

Finally, national security experts have roundly criticized the January 27 Executive Order on Terrorism as actually being detrimental to national security. The Executive Order places an immediate ban on entry from seven countries, ostensibly for security reasons. Yet, there are zero cases of nationals from the seven banned countries killing US citizens in domestic terrorist attacks between 1975 and 2015. The Executive Order also places a ban on resettlement of refugees from Syria, despite the fact that zero US citizens have been killed in terrorist attacks by Syrian refugees, and that the chance of any American citizen dying in a terrorist attack committed by a refugee is one in 3.6 billion. The Executive Order also implies that current vetting procedures for refugees are inadequate. Current vetting procedures for refugees however include multi-agency checks and last up to two years.

Furthermore, the provisions of the Executive Order actually interfere with existing US military operations against the so-called Islamic State and have sparked outrage within both the Pentagon and the State Department and Foreign Service.

If the Executive Orders on migration and security were designed as policy documents, they have completely failed. They show a lack of understanding of existing policy and have put forth measures that have been openly opposed by law enforcement officials, the Pentagon, the State Department and counterterrorism officials. Given that the Executive Orders could potentially waste billions of US tax payers' dollars to address non-existent problems—not to mention other potentially detrimental effects such as fostering domestic divisions, creating long-lasting reputational damage to the country, and harming national security, one has to question whether the Executive Orders were designed in good faith to be policy documents. If they are, it suggests a deeply worrying level of incompetence in the administration. If they are not, it suggests that the new administration is knowingly politicizing issues of national security.

Executive Orders as Political Theater

A second way to understand the President's Executive Orders is to view them not as policy instruments but rather as a form of political theater. In this reading, the purpose of the Executive Orders is not to address issues of border control or national security, but rather to signal to Trump's voter base. They are primarily symbolic gestures designed to provide the appearance of taking bold action and to give an impression of delivering on Trump's campaign promises. In other words, they are a form of political opportunism and political stunt.

There is indeed good evidence that this is a better understanding of the intended function of the Executive Orders on migration and security. The Executive Orders were hastily put together without consultation with relevant lawmakers or government agencies—there appears to have been little interest in ensuring that they addressed existing policy needs or gaps, or that they were legally and politically actionable. Indeed, the roll-out of the entry ban appears to have been deliberately dramatic and theatrical. There is absolutely no evidence that the Executive Order was responding in any shape or fashion to a plausible security threat.

The Executive Order on Terrorism was implemented in an abrupt and draconian manner—leading to the detention of children, students, professionals, the elderly and lawful permanent residents. Other than gross incompetence, the only possible explanation for this approach is that the administration engaged in a deliberate attempt to use the Executive Order as a form of political theater—to create drama, generate widespread fear and panic, and produce a reaction and backlash that could produce further polarization in a way that would benefit the administration—what some scholars have termed a "shock event." If this is the case, it should be cause for grave concern, because it suggests that the Trump administration is willing to place political considerations over policy competence on issues of national security and domestic stability. While it was clear throughout the Trump campaign that much of the rhetoric was based on political opportunism, the fact that this approach is spilling over into the process of governance represents an alarming development.

Executive Orders as Ideological Pivot

Finally, there is an additional interpretation of the Executive Orders, which is that they are not about addressing issues of national security, or even an act of political opportunism, but rather serve a broader ideological purpose. The drafting of the Executive Orders was overseen by Stephen Bannon, the ex-*Breitbart* White House strategist who is widely seen as promoting an anti-immigrant, anti-Muslim ethno-nationalist agenda. Bannon, along with White House advisor Stephen Miller, has been associated with white supremacist groups and far right nationalist and identitarian movements often referred to as the "alt-right."

A number of provisions in the Executive Orders support the interpretation that they are primarily about ideology. The Executive Order on Public Safety requires the publication of a weekly list of crimes committed by undocumented immigrants. It is hard to see the concrete public benefit of any such initiative, other than to purposefully stoke anti-immigrant sentiment within the United States—a highly undesirable outcome that could lead to a rise in hate crimes, conflict between different segments of the population, and even domestic political instability.

There are also a number of worrisome elements in the Executive Order on Terrorism that appear deliberately provocative. The Executive Order targets only Muslim-majority countries and appears to have been designed as a way of legally implementing the "Muslim Ban" that Trump called for during his election campaign. In addition, the Executive Orders introduce a religious bias into US migration policy by explicitly giving preference to religious minorities when determining refugee status. This is a move that de facto privileges Christian refugees—a provision that has been touted by Trump himself and has been criticized by numerous Christian leaders in both the United States and the affected regions.

Overall, this suggests a more "civilizational" approach to migration and national security policy—one that prioritizes ethno-religious forms of national identity. This would be a significant break from the past. Both George W. Bush and Barack Obama frequently went to great lengths to decouple Islam from terrorism and to reiterate that the United States is a multicultural society based on openness and tolerance. The Trump administration however has gone out of its way to do the opposite. It avoids any reference to liberal principles such as civil rights, human rights norms, freedom of the press, or the values of an open society. Indeed, it has quite flagrantly challenged many of these basic principles by openly calling for religious discrimination and displaying a disregard for basic norms of tolerance and civility. If the Executive Orders are indicative of a broader governing philosophy characterized by a racialized illiberalism veering into authoritarianism, we should all be very worried indeed.

In short, one is left with three possible interpretations of President Trump's Executive Orders on migration and security: as policy incompetence; political opportunism; or an ideological pivot towards a new "civilizational" security agenda. Any of these three explanations on their own should raise alarm bells; together they are cause for deep and grave concern about the new administration's approach to safeguarding national security.

Trump Unveils Harsh Illegal Immigration Enforcement Goals

Marcelo Rochabrun and Ginger Thompson

Marcelo Rochabrun is a reporting fellow with ProPublica. He recently graduated from Princeton University. Ginger Thompson is a senior reporter at ProPublica and a Pulitzer Prize winner.

Buried deep in the Trump administration's plans to round up undocumented immigrants is a provision certain to enrage Mexico—new authority for federal agents to deport anyone caught crossing the southern border to Mexico, regardless of where they are from.

If present immigration trends continue, that could mean the United States would push hundreds of thousands of Guatemalans, Hondurans, Salvadorans, Brazilians, Ecuadorans, even Haitians into Mexico. Currently, such people are detained in the U.S. and allowed to request asylum. President Trump wants them to do so from Mexico, communicating via videoconference calls with U.S. immigration officials from facilities that Mexico would presumably be forced to build.

"This would say if you want to make a claim for asylum or whatever we'll hear your case but you are going to wait in Mexico," a DHS official said. "Those are details that are being worked out both within the department and between the US government and the government of Mexico ... there are elements that still need to be worked out in detail.

John Kelly and Secretary of State Rex Tillerson will travel to Mexico later this week to meet with representatives of the Mexican government. It remains unclear if they will discuss this issue.

"Trump Plan: Deport to Mexico Immigrants Crossing Border Illegally, Regardless of Nationality," by Ginger Thompson and Marcelo Rochabrun, ProPublica, February 20, 2017. Reprinted by permission.

The new authority for immigration agents is among the dramatic, some would say untenable, tactics the Trump administration is preparing to deploy as it upends President Obama's policies on illegal immigration.

A pair of memos signed by John Kelly, the Homeland Security secretary, and publicly released on Tuesday outline the plans for what present and former government officials say will be a massive roundup of undocumented immigrants. Near final drafts of the memos had leaked over the weekend and had been first reported by McClatchy.

Officials disclosed that two former Senate aides to Attorney General Jeff Sessions drafted the plan without input from career DHS policy staffers. The ideas aren't new. Many of the approaches described in the memos come from a 1996 law that policy makers and law enforcement agents had disregarded as either unenforceable or absurd.

"Most of these provisions of law have been there for decades," the DHS official said. "We are simply trying to execute what Congress has asked us to do."

Among them was the Mexico part of the plan, for example, which calls for returning undocumented immigrants "to the foreign contiguous territory from which they arrived." The memo goes on to point out how foisting the immigrants onto Mexico would benefit DHS's budget, saying that it would, "save the Department's detention and adjudication resources for other priority aliens."

However, former senior Mexican and American immigration officials said it could very well create new security problems along the border, as authorities in each country push unwanted migrants back and forth.

The American Immigration Lawyers Association said that the proposal would violate U.S. law and international treaty obligations. Mexico is as likely to embrace the plan as it did the notion of paying for a wall. "I would expect Mexico to respond with an emphatic

'No,'" said Gustavo Mohar, a former senior Mexican immigration and national security policy official.

Whether viable or not, the Trump administration's deportation plans mark a dramatic departure from decades of policy and practice. Current and former immigration policy officials say that while the details of how the administration intends to carry out the plans remain unclear—if not insurmountable—the administration's overall message to enforcement agents across the country is clear: the limits have been lifted.

President Obama attempted to focus enforcement efforts on immigrants who had been convicted of serious crimes, and on those who were caught while or shortly after illegally entering the country. Still, his administration deported record numbers of immigrants, most of whom had only been accused of minor crimes and immigration violations.

The Trump administration says it, too, is focused on deporting criminals, but it has redefined crimes to include any activity that might bring a conviction, including entering the U.S. without permission. Effectively, that makes virtually everyone in the U.S. without a proper visa subject to roundup at their workplace or home.

"If you are present in the U.S. without being admitted or paroled or having overstayed your visa, the immigration laws of the U.S. subject you to removal," the DHS official said. "Everyone who is in violation of the laws is theoretically subject to enforcement. The Department has limited resources and we will, to the extent that we can, focus on folks who have committed serious crimes."

The only clear exception, according to the enforcement plan and the DHS briefing, is for immigrants who were illegally brought to the U.S. as children, known as Dreamers.

"Anyone who complained about Obama as the deporter-in-chief," said David Martin, formerly DHS's principal deputy general counsel, "is unfortunately going to get a taste of what it's like when someone is really gung-ho."

Greg Chen, the policy director at AILA, said the Trump plan would "effectively unleash a massive deportation force with extremely broad authority to use detention as the default mechanism for anyone suspected of violating immigration law."

The question looming over the proposals is how many of them, with all their legal and logistical obstacles, will the president actually be able to carry out.

The memos, for example, authorize the Border Patrol to hire 5,000 new agents, even though the force has never been able to fill the slots it has already been allotted. Some 60 percent of applicants to the Border Patrol fail the required polygraph, and those who pass take 18 months to get sent out into the field.

The Trump plan calls for the expansion of a George W. Bush-era program, known as 287g, which allows DHS to deputize state and local police as immigration agents. It was touted after 9/11 as a critical "force-multiplier." But by 2010, some of the country's largest police departments were refusing to participate because they believed it would shatter the trust between their officers and the communities they were sworn to protect. Meanwhile, participating agencies, which foot the bill for the program, were suddenly saddled with new debts and hounded by accusations of racial profiling and other abuse, forcing the Obama administration to suspend expansion of the program.

Until now, the enforcement of summary deportation laws, known as "expedited removal," have been limited to those apprehended within 14 days of illegally entering the country and within 100 miles of Canada or Mexico. The memos signed by Kelly would allow use of those laws anywhere in the country against anyone who entered illegally within the past two years.

Lucas Guttentag, a former DHS adviser and Stanford law professor, said this would "unleash chaos," violate due process, and meet challenges in court, similar to those that scuttled the administration's travel ban.

There would also be aggressive challenges, lawyers said, to plans that would allow immigration agents to deport unaccompanied minor children who crossed the border illegally, rather than uniting them with parents or other relatives in the U.S.

The reason for discussing unaccompanied minors is "that they have been abandoned by their parents or legal guardians," the DHS official said. If it is "determined that there is a parent or guardian in the U.S. that they can be handed over to, then DHS needs to take a hard look over whether that person is actually" an unaccompanied minor.

"There will be a renewed focus on ensuring that folks don't abuse the system," the DHS official added.

They also expect legal opposition to a proposal that would strip undocumented immigrants of existing privacy protections, allowing personal information such as asylum cases or immigration violations to be publicly disclosed.

"We want to ensure that our privacy policies are consistent with the law," the DHS official said. "The Privacy Act applies by statute to citizens" and green card holders. "The President has asked us to align our laws with what congress has directed."

"The Trump people have clearly bought into the model of harsh enforcement. They apparently think, 'we'll be tough, and a lot of people will leave on their own,'" said Martin, an immigration law professor at the University of Virginia. "They believe they'll win in the court of public opinion. I'm not sure about that. A lot of Americans know hard-working undocumented immigrants. The kind of enforcement Trump's people are talking about will visibly create many more sympathetic cases than unsympathetic ones."

Some of the provisions explicitly acknowledge that it could take years before DHS has the manpower and money to pull off what the president has ordered. Immigration enforcement agents, however, have already begun filling the policy void by launching raids and deportations, including some that advocates worry are meant to test the limits. Meanwhile panic has taken hold in many immigrant communities.

"The level of fear is more than anything we've ever seen," said Marielena Hincapie, executive director of the National Immigration

Law Center. She said the plan's sweep, "sent a chill to my bones," because it threatens to do irreparable harm to millions of families. She added, "This all seems aimed at changing who we are as a nation."

Update, Feb. 21, 2017: In a call with reporters Tuesday morning, DHS officials confirmed they were working on a plan to send migrants who had entered the United States from Mexico back to Mexico, even if they were not citizens of that country.

Opponents of Trump's Executive Orders on Immigration Are Overreacting

Sarah Birnbaum

Sarah Birnbaum is a Boston-based reporter. She was formerly in Cape Town, South Africa, and previously served as WGBH Radio's political and state house reporter.

This is just a temporary pause. That's the point," Mark Krikorian says. "This isn't the policy about how we're going to screen people coming from countries where there are active jihad terror groups."

Krikorian is the executive director of the right-leaning Center for Immigration Studies, a think tank. He is one of the leading intellectual architects of the movement to restrict immigration to the United States.

Trump's executive order bans the Syrian refugee program indefinitely. It suspends immigration for 90 days from Iran, Iraq, Libya, Somalia, Sudan, and Yemen. It also suspends the US program for admitting refugees from anywhere in the world for 120 days, while the government comes up with a stricter process for vetting them.

The process to gaining permission to enter the US can already be time-consuming. For Syrians and other refugees, it's especially difficult. The US has accepted very few of the nearly 5 million Syrians who have fled their homes since the war there started in 2011.

In fiscal year 2014, the US only accepted 105 Syrians. In 2015, that number was 1,682 and in 2016 the US resettled 12,587 Syrians. The vetting process can take 18 to 24 months for Syrians. Fewer than 1 percent of applicants make it through the initial screening by the United Nations Refugee Agency, which is required before the US will consider them.

"Why This Think Tank Director Supports Trump's Immigration Ban," by Sarah Birnbaum, Public Radio International, January 31, 2017. Reprinted by permission.

Krikorian says it makes sense to suspend the refugee program, at least in the short term, so the administration "can figure out whether the screening we do now is appropriate or needs to be tightened. ... This isn't an indication of what the actual policy three or four months from now will be."

The order allows for exceptions for persecuted religious minorities, like Christians in Muslim countries.

Krikorian insists that it does not represent a "Muslim ban," as many opponents have characterized it. He says that the seven Muslim-majority countries named in the order were already listed as "countries of concern" when Congress passed the "Terrorist Travel Prevention Act" in 2015. Krikorian points to the fact that Muslims from other nations, like Indonesia and Saudi Arabia, are still allowed to enter the US. "If, in three months from now, there's a policy that says anybody who fasts during Ramadan shouldn't come into the United States ... well that's ridiculous and I'll be against it then," he says.

Homeland Security Secretary John Kelly said in a press briefing Tuesday that the order is a "temporary pause," not a ban. But, he said, "Some of these countries won't be getting off the list any time soon," especially those "in various states of collapse." Kelly also said the department may work with other countries not named in the executive order—though some officials have suggested the list of banned countries could be expanded—to gain more information about people coming into the US.

While experts have called the ban a gift to ISIS recruitment, Krikorian blames the media, not Trump, for feeding jihadi propaganda. Krikorian says journalists have insisted on mislabeling the ban. "The news coverage of this is helping ISIS," he insists. "Describing it in shorthand as a Muslim ban—or even taking that description seriously—is more likely to be helping ISIS than the actual policy."

In the end, Krikorian says the backlash against the immigration order is "hyperbolic," especially given what he considers the relatively small number of people detained.

White House Press Secretary Sean Spicer said on Monday that only 109 people out of 325,000 were stopped for additional screening after Trump's order. But news reports have proven those numbers to be false. The Daily Beast reports that 735 people who had encounters with border officials could have been barred from entering the United States, while the *Washington Post* puts the number of people affected by Trump's travel ban at 90,000—accounting for everyone from the seven banned countries who received a US visa in 2015.

Krikorian says he's heard the dramatic stories of refugees blocked from returning to school or reuniting with relatives after the ban. He says he feels sorry for them, but ultimately, he shrugs it off. "Of course, it's going to create inconveniences for people," Krikorian says. "Still, no foreign citizen has any right to come to the United States. None whatsoever."

Some travelers with valid documents to enter the US have been questioned and held for up to 24 hours, often without access to lawyers. Others, refugees and people who have worked with the US military, are waiting for their chance to leave dangerous circumstances in order to start life in the US.

Trump Administration Criminalizes Migrants

Teresa Gutierrez

Activist Teresa Gutierrez is a writer and leader in the Workers World Party. She was the WWP's vice presidential nominee in 2004.

Ultra-racists and warmongers like Donald Trump, Jeff Sessions, John Kelly and their Immigration and Customs Enforcement agents are setting Washington's immigration agenda on behalf of the capitalist system.

This is intensifying the modern war to criminalize migrants in the United States that began in 2006. But it is a war that will ultimately be won by the unity of all the working class, whether foreign- or U.S.-born.

This war against immigrants is not separate from the government-Pentagon drive to imperialist war in Syria or North Korea. In fact, U.S. intervention abroad is a major cause of forced migration.

Washington is taking a very dangerous, threatening posture against revolutionary Venezuela as well. It is similar to when President Barack Obama and Secretary of State Hillary Clinton orchestrated a coup in Honduras in 2009, which created further forced migration from that country.

The U.S. immigration issue is also critically linked to the refugee crisis in Europe. While the U.S. drops missiles in Syria on the pretext of caring for children, the Trump administration hypocritically refuses to admit Syrian refugees, including children, into this country.

Most Syrian refugees go to the countries of western Europe, which is also the destination of vast masses of migrants from other countries in the Middle East, North Africa and Eastern Europe.

Conditions for these refugees in Europe are as bad as those for migrants on the U.S./Mexican border.

The war on migrants and the migrants' plight, whether in the U.S. or Europe, is deeply connected to every struggle, whether it's the fight against climate change or the cutbacks looming in Medicaid or the struggle for health care, union rights and education. It is connected to the Black Lives Matter movement as Black immigrants and/or Muslims are disproportionately targeted.

DHS Headed by Southcom General

The Department of Homeland Security's website states that it "has a vital mission: to secure the nation from the many threats we face."

The current secretary of the DHS is John Kelly, a retired general who spent 45 years in the armed forces.

On April 18, Kelly spoke at George Washington University. An April 21 *New York Times* editorial summed up his remarks as fear mongering: "The tone he sets can only encourage abusive behavior among his officers ... against immigrants, and also lead to the curtailment of civil liberties and privacy."

It adds that his "apocalyptic talk turns the Islamophobia and immigrant scapegoating that turbocharged the Trump campaign into marching orders for federal law enforcement agents and bureaucrats."

Kelly's history is key to understanding his role today. He is a warmonger, one of those responsible for the criminal destruction and countless deaths in Iraq.

He is a former head of the U.S. Southern Command, which includes Guantánamo Bay in Cuba, illegally occupied by the Pentagon and used for the last 16 years as a torture prison for people kidnapped from other countries and held without rights or trial.

As head of the Southern Command, Kelly was also deeply involved with all U.S. military activities in South and Central America in the 1980s.

That was an important period in Central American history.

Nicaraguans, Guatemalans, Salvadorans and Hondurans were fighting heroic, important revolutionary battles to free themselves from colonial and imperialist domination.

Had they been allowed to control their own destinies, we would not see the forced migration of today.

Now John Kelly is working nonstop to deport as many Central Americans as possible back to certain death and misery. And he continues Trump's racist, dangerous Islamophobia that attempts to blame Muslims for every act of terror.

Kelly is also a strong proponent of keeping the Guantánamo Bay prison open at all costs. Human-rights investigators from the United Nations and other agencies proved that prisoners, especially Muslims, have been held there in violation of their human and civil rights.

In fact, the Center for Constitutional Rights, which has led the legal fight against Guantánamo and represented some of the detainees, stated that Kelly's "aggressive oversight of the illegal military prison ... disqualifies him" from leading DHS.

News accounts report that Kelly supports waterboarding.

"Presiding over a population of detainees not charged or convicted of crimes, Kelly treated them with brutality," CCR reported. "His response to the detainees' peaceful hunger strike in 2013 was punitive force-feeding, solitary confinement, and rubber bullets. Furthermore, he sabotaged efforts by the Obama administration to resettle detainees."

This is the person now sending ICE agents to the homes of workers who only want to put food on their families' tables.

Money for People, Not Concentration Camps

During last year's election campaign, Trump promised that immigration would be a cornerstone of his administration. He is carrying out that promise.

The Trump administration is assembling a vast deportation force whose policies are being carried out by ICE agents who have publicly expressed their hatred of immigrants.

The Washington Post reported on April 12 that it had

obtained an internal DHS assessment memo that revealed that the department has secured 33,000 more detention beds to house immigrants. These detention sites evoke the heinous period of Japanese internment camps in the 1940s.

Detentions are only one part of the rapidly enforced immigration policies carried out by the Trump administration. DHS is working closer than ever with local police forces, which are being empowered to carry out ICE roles. It is fast-tracking ways to hire more ICE agents and may even end polygraph and physical fitness tests for them. This opens up the possibility of hiring more thug-like agents than ever before.

Deportations will increase under Trump. Immediately on taking office he signed executive orders that expanded the pool of undocumented and even documented migrants to be singled out as a priority for removal.

An April 16 *New York Post* report on Kelly said that "under the Trump administration's tougher immigration rules, even a 'single DUI' can start the deportation process."

This means that a migrant stopped on the road can be easily put into the system, detained and deported.

It gets worse.

What was once a routine check-in for the undocumented has now become a day of terror. Before the Trump era, DHS officers had applied "prosecutorial discretion," leading to more so-called convicted criminals being deported, while those without a criminal record just checked in every year.

That has changed. Now many walk into court for their annual check-in and do not walk out. So being undocumented is itself now being treated as a crime.

The immigrant rights movement points out that the rhetoric about "criminal" or "noncriminal" immigrants is a divisive wedge issue—and is rightly demanding the end of deportations of ALL immigrants, criminal record or not, and permanent residency for all undocumented workers. These workers and their families have certainly earned it.

Ultra-Racist Sessions Now Top Lawyer

Attorney General Jeff Sessions visited the U.S.-Mexican border at Nogales, Ariz., on April 11. The purpose of the trip was to announce policies to step up the government's prosecution of undocumented workers, policies that affect documented migrants as well.

In Sessions' written statement he called the policies a "move against filth like gangs and criminal aliens."

When Sessions was appointed attorney general, it stunned anti-racists and civil rights leaders. "That means a man with white supremacist ties, a racist and homophobic legislative record, and a history of opposing voting rights is now the top law enforcement officer in the country," wrote Think Progress on Feb. 8.

In 1986 Sessions was denied a judgeship after testimony on his support for the Ku Klux Klan. Democrats have noted that Sessions is more anti-immigrant than anyone else in Congress.

Sessions said on the border: "This is a new era. This is the Trump era. The lawlessness, the abdication of the duty to enforce our immigration laws, and the catch-and-release practices of old are over."

A parent who brings children over the border can now be charged with "harboring," sent to jail and deported. Nonviolent immigrants who enter the country illegally for a second time will be charged with a felony, not a misdemeanor as previously.

Sessions is calling for charging workers with "document fraud" and "aggravated identify theft."

An anonymous federal prosecutor told the Daily Beast that the new directives are "generating widespread negative response" and called them "f***ing horrifying." (commondreams.org, April 12)

Stop Racist Deportations and Islamophobia! Permanent Residency for All Migrants!

The Trump administration directives are a further call to war on migrants, meant to paint all immigrants as threats and criminals. The administration wants people to think Muslims are all terrorists.

These moves to appease far-right anti-immigrant elements are part of an overall racist campaign to push back the gains that workers of color have made through militant struggle. The goal is to divide and conquer the working class.

But the real terrorists are the white supremacists and warmongers now running Washington. A "Blue Lives Matter" ideology is pushing policy that means more war here at home and abroad.

This makes the May Day 2017 strike much more important—and the struggles for migrant and worker rights that will go on after May Day that much more decisive.

More than ever our movements in the streets—whether for immigrant rights, against police terror, to stop wars abroad and climate change, for women's or LGBTQ rights—must become anti-capitalist as well as internationalist.

We must show not only in slogans but in our actions that there are no borders in the workers' struggle, that we stand united with workers in every country, from every country. Our lives depend on it.

Trump Lacks Mandate for Immigration Overhaul

Mae Ngai

Mae M. Ngai is an American historian and Lung Family professor of Asian American studies and professor of history at Columbia University.

We all know what Donald Trump promised he'd do on immigration, ever since he launched his campaign in 2015 with a declaration of war against Mexican immigrants, whom he shockingly branded as rapists and criminals. The famous promise to build a wall ("big and beautiful") along the southern border, paid for by Mexico. A "deportation task force" to rid the country of 11 million undocumented immigrants, and possibly legal ones too, the criminals and "bad hombres." Ban Muslims from entering the country, or people from countries with large Muslim populations, or make all Muslims in the United States register. Cancel on day one all of President Obama's executive orders, including the DACA (Deferred Action for Childhood Arrivals) program, in effect since 2012, that has given reprieve from deportation to some 750,000 young people who came to the United States as children. The specter of raids and round-ups in factories, fields and communities, of college students yanked out of their classes, of the Statue of Liberty replaced with a thirty-foot by 2000-mile wall as the nation's message to immigrants—the horror of it is breathtaking.

Trump has a documented history of racism against African Americans that goes back to the 1970s, when his buildings refused to rent to black people. But he seems to have had much less of a history of xenophobia, notwithstanding his racial antipathy towards Latinos. Nativism exists in New York City but it is not prominent,

"A Call for Sanctuary," by Mae Ngai, *Dissent* Magazine, November 22, 2016. Reprinted by permission.

despite the spike in hate crimes it has witnessed since the election. We are, after all, America's quintessential city of immigrants. They are the entrepreneurs, professionals, workers, and artists, who drive and animate city life.

Trump's embrace of nativism was not just another box to check for a conservative campaign. It was a cold calculus to put protectionism—"immigration" twinned with "unfair trade" (especially from Mexico and China)—at the center of a strategy to stoke the resentment of white working-class and lower-middle-class people left behind by globalization. Other aspects of Trump's campaign strategy, notably the misogynistic demonization of Clinton, fed the central narrative of protectionism. Clinton was the face of Washington elitism and corruption, the establishment that had forsaken American jobs. It all worked, to stunning effect.

Will the new administration deliver on its immigration promises? At the time of this writing Trump has not yet appointed a secretary for Homeland Security, the federal agency responsible for immigration enforcement. His first appointments—Jeff Sessions for Attorney General, General Mike Flynn as national security adviser, and Mike Pompeo as head of the CIA—are on the right-wing extreme of the Republican spectrum. We can expect a hardliner at Homeland Security, too. Nevertheless, it will be difficult for the administration to carry out Trump's full immigration agenda. Congress will balk at funding the Wall (estimated cost $25 billion) and deporting 11 million people (upwards of $400 billion). Trump has already begun dialing back from Wall to fence and a pledge to prioritize the deportation of 2-3 million "criminal aliens." Even if he does not implement these measures, we can surely expect more immigration raids of workplaces and farms and heightened surveillance of communities. A few spectacular raids will play to the nativist base. And even if most undocumented people are not actually deported, they will all live in fear, even more fear than they experience now. Some might decide to leave on their own (or "self-deport," as Mitt Romney advocated in 2012).

It remains to be seen if Trump will revoke DACA, which would affect 750,000 undocumented young people who are now able to attend college, lawfully work, hold driver's licenses, open bank accounts, and travel. Unlike some of Trump's proposals, which require congressional approval and appropriation, DACA can be canceled with the stroke of a pen. But it is also politically risky. DACA holders are highly visible and appealing to the public on account of their youth, the innocence of their undocumented status, and their aspirations for education, jobs, and careers. They are the "dreamers" who, more than any other group, won public support for legalization and a path to citizenship for the undocumented. Their persistent organizing resulted in President Obama's executive action that created DACA after the Republicans blocked immigration reform in the Congress, as well as a second executive order, Deferred Action for Parents of Americans. But DAPA was never implemented, owing to court challenges and injunctions.

In the days after the election, DACA students were stunned and shaken by the prospect of losing their status. At my institution, Columbia University, the dangers they face had palpable effect. They cried in our classrooms and bravely spoke out in public of their vulnerability. Will they be able to continue their education? What will happen if they lose their work authorization? Can they go home for the holidays or return to campus if they lose the authorization to travel? Will they or their parents be deported? But at Columbia, as at so many other schools, they have also sprung into action. They have galvanized support from their fellow students and professors, spurring university and college presidents to issue statements that their institutions will protect them. In addition, on November 21, the presidents of 180 colleges and universities issued a statement in support of DACA. "To our country's leaders, we say that DACA should be upheld, continued and expanded," the statement reads. "This is both a moral imperative and a national necessity."

Meanwhile, student/faculty petitions asking universities to declare themselves sanctuaries have garnered thousands of signatures. Already, some twenty universities have responded with either full declarations of sanctuary or other declarations that do not use the word *sanctuary* but pledge non-cooperation with immigration enforcement, specifically prohibiting immigration agents from entering campuses and refusing to share information about students' status, unless forced by warrants or court order. These include the entire California State University system (where there are an estimated 10,000 undocumented students), Portland State University, Rutgers, Yale, Brown, Pomona, Reed, and my own institution, Columbia, among others.

The campus sanctuary movement builds on a history of solidarity dating back to the Underground Railroad and northern refusal to comply with fugitive slave laws. In more recent years, local governments have established explicit and de-facto immigration sanctuaries. These entail a range of non-cooperation policies: Local law enforcement, for example, can refuse to cooperate with immigration raids and ICE's "detainer" policy (detaining and handing over undocumented persons stopped or arrested by local law enforcement, including for traffic violations and misdemeanors). Or city employees and agencies can be prohibited from asking a person their immigration status in the course of conducting normal city business. Today, some form of sanctuary policy exists in thirty-nine cities and more than 200 counties across the country. They are not just in the liberal northeast and Pacific coast but also in Florida, Kansas, North Dakota, Louisiana, Colorado, Georgia, and other states. No county jail in New Mexico will honor ICE detainer policy.

New York has been a sanctuary city since 1989, when Mayor Ed Koch issued an executive order of non-cooperation with immigration enforcement. His successors have continued the policy, including Rudy Giuliani, who defended it in court and, when he lost on appeal, continued it in defiance. Mayor Bill de Blasio has reiterated the city's commitment to its sanctuary policy (as well as protection of Muslims and women's reproductive rights). He is one of eleven mayors who affirmed their sanctuary policies in the last weeks. They know they are gearing up for a fight: Trump said he would stop federal block grants to sanctuary cities if elected. Public support and official steadfastness will have to make sure he doesn't deliver on the threat.

And they have the power to. Deportation on a mass scale is not possible without cooperation from local authorities. City and county governments and institutions such as universities and churches can block a deportation drive. Churches are especially important because they may provide the only source of sanctuary for migrant workers in non-urban areas. Here, then, is an opportunity, indeed an imperative, for all people of conscience to defend our neighbors, coworkers, student peers, and co-congregants who are threatened with deportation.

The American public does not support mass removal of immigrants. Trump does not have a mandate to build a wall, to deport millions of people, to cancel DACA. This is where we draw a line in the sand. We have the power to resist and refuse—and to stop it.

CHAPTER 4

Are Immigrant and Deportation Policies Headed in the Right Direction?

Overview: Rhetoric Versus Reality in Trump's Immigration Policies

Susan Ferriss

Susan Ferriss is a prize-winning former foreign correspondent who has been investigating the treatment of children by the US justice and immigration system, law enforcement, and the school-discipline process.

During a Republican primary debate last February, Sen. Marco Rubio of Florida seized a moment. He asserted that even though Donald Trump the candidate was attacking undocumented immigrants, Trump the businessman had used 200 undocumented Polish workers to build Trump Towers, the president-elect's gilded Gotham high-rise.

This foreign-worker imbroglio involving Trump—there are more—led to a court ruling in 1991 that Trump associates were in on a plan to stiff a laborers' union out of pension benefits by underpaying the Poles. Trump professed not to know about the workers' status, according to reports, and he appealed. Fifteen years later, though, after some of the Poles went public in news reports about wage and safety violations, Trump ended the protracted legal battle with a sealed settlement.

"He brings up something from 30 years ago," Trump said at the debate, lashing back at Rubio. Trump said laws were different then. "It worked out very well," he said with a shrug. "Everybody was happy."

But millions of Americans who are married or otherwise related to other undocumented people are not at all happy today—and they can't afford to shrug off the past like Trump. Employers who have stepped up over the years to admit that many employees are likely undocumented are also dismayed. They fear that Trump's

"Trump and Immigration: Tough Talk Masks a Complex Reality," by Susan Ferriss, the Center for Public Integrity, December 12, 2016. Reprinted by permission.

election means the end of a long quest for immigration reform that recognizes that most undocumented workers are not the "criminals" or "bad hombres" that Trump excoriated during the campaign. Instead, they're the spouses and parents of U.S. citizens, longtime co-workers and neighbors and home and business owners—and their issues, problems and challenges are far more complex than Trump's heated rhetoric would make it appear.

A Chill in the Air

"Our members are scared out of their wits," said Kim Anderson, a Minnesotan who leads American Families United. The group represents U.S. citizens with undocumented spouses who are unable to legalize those spouses under current immigration laws without great risks. Members are now coming to grips with the possibility that their circumstances are about to get even worse.

On immigration, like on many other subjects, it's sometimes hard to figure where the president-elect's bluster ends and his actual position lies. Trump's stinging words about Mexicans and Muslims during the campaign are old news, but not forgotten as he prepares to take power. He initiated his campaign by fixating on Mexicans who cross the border, calling them "rapists" before adding, after a pause, that "some, I assume, are good people." He tried softening his rhetoric in an Arizona speech by referring to "the great contributions of Mexican-American citizens to our two countries … and the close friendship between our two nations." But Trump's appointment of Steve Bannon as his chief White House strategist has inflamed tensions further because of Bannon's talk-radio past and his Breitbart website, which features diatribes degrading immigrants and people of color.

For members of American Families United, the prospects their concerns will be heard feel thin.

A myth persists that if Americans marry undocumented people—who many have met at work—those spouses can easily transition to legal status. The reality is that Americans can no longer apply to get green cards for undocumented spouses without facing severe consequences if their husbands or wives originally entered the country illegally and were here for more than one year. Those spouses are automatically subject to being banished from the United States for 10 years, sometimes longer, even for life. This policy came about long before Trump; a Republican-controlled Congress tucked the punitive measures, known as bars, into the 1996 Illegal Immigration Reform and Immigrant Responsibility Act. Application of the bars was phased in, shocking a first wave of couples who were unaware of the changes.

More than 9 million people appear to live in "mixed status" families with an undocumented adult and at least one U.S.-born child, according to the Pew Research Center. As of 2014, Pew estimated, 66 percent of undocumented adults had been in the United States for more than 10 years—enough time to form families.

Because of the rules, some mixed-status families have already been forced into exile to stay intact. They've suffered financial strain and emotional trauma. Others, to keep jobs here, have had to live separately from spouses and children who are stuck abroad, as the Center for Public Integrity reported in 2012. Still others have chosen not even to try for green cards and instead live every day worrying that a spouse could get picked up in a workplace raid or due to a traffic stop.

For years, these citizens have tried to persuade Congress unsuccessfully to reform these penalties—arguing that the bars have done nothing to deter illegal immigration and instead are a disproportionate punishment falling on Americans. Multiple bills with some bipartisan support have so far stalled in Congress.

President Obama's administration did make a slight change that's aided some in this community; in 2013 he issued a regulatory tweak allowing spouses seeking green cards to apply for waivers from banishment *without* having to leave the country, as had been required. However, since many spouses had already been advised they would not qualify for the narrow criteria for a waiver, they were unable to benefit from the regulatory change.

"Our members have lived in this unknown fear for years that at any given moment their lives can be wrecked, irreversibly," Alexander said. With Trump's election, "that's been ratcheted up by 10 times."

Hard-Line Approach

Indeed, Trump's position sounds uncompromising.

"For those here today illegally who are seeking legal status, they will have one route and only one route: to return home and apply for re-entry," Trump said in his Arizona speech. "Our message to the world will be this: You cannot obtain legal status, or become a citizen of the United States, by illegally entering our country."

Another group whose future now appears in peril: more than 700,000 so-called "Dreamers," young people whose parents brought them here as children and whom President Obama and a number of Republican leaders have defended as Americans in all but documents. So-called DREAM Act legislation that would have provided Dreamers an earned path to legal status has failed repeatedly. So in 2012, Obama issued an executive order granting some Dreamers who registered with the government temporary protection from deportation and two-year work permits that must be renewed.

Obama has urged Trump to show compassion for Dreamers. "It is my strong belief that the majority of the American people would not want to see suddenly those kids have to start hiding again," Obama said. But Trump has said he'll "immediately terminate" Obama executive orders like the Dreamer policy. He's also said that only after the border is controlled "will we be in a position to consider the appropriate disposition of those who remain."

In an interview with *TIME* magazine this month, Trump suggested "we're going to work something out" for Dreamers. They "got brought here at a very young age, they've worked here, they've gone to school here," he said. "Some were good students. Some have wonderful jobs. And they're in never-never land because they don't know what's going to happen."

One of Congress' hardliners, Rep. Steve King, R-Iowa, didn't sound happy with the softer tone. He told CNN that "among these Dreamers are some awfully bad people," and he added: "Will those children point to their parents and tell us, 'You really need to enforce the law against my parents, because they knew what they were doing when they caused me to break the law?'"

A circle of immigration-restriction activists who favor a tough line—and who say they've advised the Trump campaign—have historically expressed little mercy for Dreamers.

When a version of the DREAM Act failed to pass in 2007, Roy Beck, the executive director of NumbersUSA, one of these groups, said he had no sympathy for the young people.

"I have no trouble looking at them in the eye and saying, 'Too bad. Life is hard,'" Beck told the *Sacramento Bee*. Beck, whose group has mobilized voters to oppose Dream Act proposals, told Reuters this fall that he met Trump in New York during the campaign.

NumbersUSA declares a policy of "no to immigrant bashing" on its website and contends its concern is over-population. But the Southern Poverty Law Center criticized the group in a report, "The Nativist Lobby: Three Faces of Intolerance," due to racially charged remarks expressed by a founder and a Beck associate.

Chris Kobach, the controversial Kansas secretary of state, has also been among those counseling Trump on immigration matters. Before he held elected office, Kobach pressed several lawsuits to deprive Dreamers of the right to pay in-state tuition to attend public colleges where they grew up. His suits have failed in California, Nebraska and Kansas.

Kobach was also the architect of an Arizona law that required police there to demand proof of legal status for people suspected of being undocumented. The U.S. Supreme Court reviewed that law and upheld the power of police to investigate a person's status under certain conditions. But as part of a civil-rights lawsuit settlement Arizona stopped requiring police to demand evidence of legal status or hold people for prolonged periods solely for that purpose.

Back in 2012, while advising GOP presidential candidate Mitt Romney, Kobach argued that within four years, if "attrition through enforcement were made the centerpiece of national immigration policy, you could see the illegal alien population cut in half." The battle of Dreamers could shift to Congress again soon: GOP Sen. Lindsey Graham of South Carolina, a longtime supporter of legal status for Dreamers, plans to introduce another version of the Dream Act next year.

Unforeseen Consequences

Regardless of what actually happens on the policy front, though, what Anderson of American Families United fears is more collateral damage.

She worries additional Americans will be driven into exile—like Margot Bruemmer. Originally from New Jersey, Bruemmer was a college English professor when she moved with her young children and undocumented husband in 2005 to Veracruz, Mexico. Bruemmer's spouse learned at a green-card interview in Mexico that he was barred from entering the United State for at least 10 years. After 10 years, the couple re-applied for the green card. But he was rejected again. A devastated Bruemmer is facing a lifetime outside the United States to keep her family together.

"Begging and pleading by phone, email, and in person with senators and congressmen was in vain," the mother of three children said in a message to friends.

Anderson questions what benefit there is for Americans "to deny life in the United States to Margot's children."

But Anderson conceded that mustering support for undocumented immigrants isn't easy. A Gallup poll last July actually found that 84 percent of U.S. adults—and 76 percent of Republicans—favored allowing undocumented immigrants to earn legal status over time if they met certain requirements. Yet Anderson acknowledged the battle cry often rising above that sentiment: that the undocumented should "do it the right way," and "get in line," and shouldn't be rewarded with legal status.

That rhetoric bumps up against a cold reality; the current immigration system doesn't actually provide a way for most undocumented people to correct their status by getting in a line. Without a change in policy, many spouses of Americans or legal residents face the punitive bars blocking them from re-entering the United States. For many others, there is no line at all: Most visas for legal residency are based on marriage or other immediate family ties. Work visa categories and opportunities for employer sponsorship for green cards are extremely narrow—benefiting mostly people with so-called "extraordinary" skills, including professional athletes and models, which is what facilitated Trump's wife Melania's transition to the United States.

Even if a U.S. employer is eager to sponsor and "legalize" undocumented workers who've become trusted workers—in farming, for example, or elder care—it's all but impossible because "unskilled" job visas are few and requests are backlogged for years. On top of that, at present, any history of crossing the border illegally or undocumented status can be disqualifying.

Americans frustrated by these barriers contrast their experiences with what they've heard about the future First Lady.

Melania Trump has said that she followed all visa rules when she arrived here about 20 years ago. But according to an Associated Press investigation, documents showed that Melania performed 10 modeling jobs valued at more than $20,000 while she was still on a visitor's visa in 1996 that did not permit her to work. The jobs were performed, the AP reported, weeks before she was issued an H-1B non-immigrant temporary work visa in October 1996. Violating terms of a visa or presenting a misleading history involving a visa can result in denial of re-entry to the United States and denial of a permanent residency application. Melania obtained permanent residency in 2001, but hasn't elaborated on how she made that transition. She became a U.S. citizen in 2006, a year after she and Trump married.

The contrast with businesses like agriculture appear stark to many—including Barry Bedwell, president of the California

Agricultural Leadership Foundation. Agribusiness leans heavily Republican, but Bedwell counts himself among those dispirited by Trump's rhetoric and worried about what comes next.

The long partnership between employers and the undocumented has been "allowed ... to develop because it's been mutually beneficial," admitted Bedwell. Like many in agribusiness, he's frustrated that conservatives in other parts of the country aren't open to his point of view. But "now that we've moved past the campaign," he said, "I'm hoping cooler heads will prevail."

Bedwell is based in the Salinas Valley, and before that he was based in Fresno—two of the most productive agribusiness regions in the world. Tending and harvesting crops must be done at precise moments in time, so workers need to be available. California has much at stake in whatever the Trump Administration does here—and so do American consumers, given that the Golden State produces the majority of America's fruits and vegetables and is the leading producer of milk—and relies heavily on undocumented laborers.

"What the agricultural community needs to do now," Bedwell said, "is understand its vulnerabilities and play extreme defense."

Troubling Stalemate

For many, both recent history and the current situation seem counterproductive. President Bill Clinton's administration began investing billions on fortifying the border in the mid-1990s, and President George W. Bush invested billions more. Smugglers' fees began escalating and trips became more dangerous, so more and more workers stayed put.

Trump argues that "lower-skilled" immigrants "compete directly against vulnerable American workers, and ... draw much more out of the system than they will ever pay in." But agribusiness companies have complained at times about worker shortages in the wake of extra border security, such as occasional deployments of the National Guard, and most economists argue that American consumers have benefited overall from immigrant labor, documented or not.

Stretching back to the 1990s, a coalition of business, labor and civil rights groups have unsuccessfully pursued reform. They didn't always agree on everything. But versions of bills they generally backed would have legalized some of the current workforce for the sake of preventing disruption in the national food supply and other industries, and to promote community and family stability. Proposals would have also overhauled the system for vetting claims of worker shortages and then admitting workers to fill jobs that aren't necessarily considered "extraordinary"—like modeling—but essential to the economy.

Proposals included trade-offs that were uncomfortable for some. Versions of farmworker-specific legislation would have phased-in a legalization of current workers, on condition they stayed in the fields for a period before leaving for other jobs. Farmers would be expected to increase use of a guest worker program whose inefficiencies they could help reform. For some labor advocates, these provisions were a bitter pill because unions fought to end the exploitative Bracero program in 1964 that had imported Mexican farmworkers without equal rights. But labor activists were also concerned that workers were dying crossing deserts for jobs, or were undocumented and less able to fight for better treatment.

Provisions in these failed immigration bills would have also poured billions of dollars more into additional border security. And in an unprecedented step, all versions of these bills would have also phased in mandatory employer use of the E-Verify system, an online system for authenticating ID documents.

To understand why employers—and labor activists—support such broad-based reforms, Bedwell and others say, Americans need a better understanding of what's happened in the past.

E-Verify didn't exist when Congress and President Ronald Reagan approved the last major immigration legislation 30 years ago—a bitterly contested measure known as the Simpson-

Mazzoli Act. Before the 1986 reform, it wasn't even illegal to hire undocumented workers. Into the 1970s, employers could sponsor undocumented immigrants for green cards with greater ease. Immigration judges, too, had greater latitude to review individual cases and grant legal status.

In 1986, in addition to an amnesty, Congress mandated that employers ask to see a prospective employee's documents indicating legal status—and then record and keep that information on file. Not complying can result in a fine. But employers aren't expected to be experts in detecting fake documents. And with rare exception, most escape responsibility for hiring undocumented workers because the legal burden of proving they "knowingly" hired workers is difficult to meet. So the employer sanctions that were part of the legislation proved largely ineffective. And even though border control spending exploded in the mid-1990s, workers willing to risk more perilous crossings kept coming, and employers kept hiring them to fill jobs—not just on farms, but in construction and services.

Now, though, mandating E-Verify would be a potential game changer for businesses—assuming the system's not insignificant operational problems can be smoothed out. Trump has said his administration "will ensure that E-Verify is used to the fullest extent possible under existing law, and will work with Congress to strengthen and expand its use across the country."

The U.S. Chamber of Commerce, which led the comprehensive-immigration-reform charge for years in Washington, has produced reams of documents featuring economists' positive take on immigration. The group points to longitudinal studies finding that immigrants boost economic growth, tax revenues and on balance push up wages for the native-born, who assume more management roles.

But since Trump's victory, the chamber has gone silent, and is regrouping for a new era. "We're not going to speculate on anything related to the Trump administration's policies at this time," a spokeswoman said in an email. "We look forward to working with the new administration and the new Congress on issues of importance to the business community, which includes immigration reform."

Swimming Upstream

Even before Trump, reform advocates like the Chamber were up against a rising tide of skepticism regarding reform.

Congress grew cold after the 9/11 terrorist attacks, and conservative talk radio and TV programs began a drumbeat of attacks against legalizing immigrants; TV personalities such as Lou Dobbs spread outlandish claims about Mexican plots to "take over" the American Southwest. Ironically, Mexican President Vicente Fox—the most pro-U.S. Mexican president in modern times—was increasingly excoriated by Dobbs and others. As wars in Afghanistan and Iraq tarnished President Bush's popularity, he lost his ability to muster GOP support for a reform he had pushed. An influx of Central Americans fleeing violent gangs also brought a backlash.

Immigrant advocates aren't convinced that Trump's pledges to get tough will result in a mass exodus of people, but they do think workers will feel pain far more than employers. Bruce Goldstein, president of the nonprofit Farmworker Justice in Washington, D.C, said, "I'm worried that the current undocumented workers will be pushed further into the margins of society where they will suffer more."

Bill Hing, a veteran immigration attorney and professor at the University of San Francisco, said his phone is "ringing off the hook now" as clients seek "an educated guess" on what Trump might do. More workplace raids might occur to "make a splash," Hing also predicted. But employers, especially agribusiness, he said, are sure to try to enlist GOP leaders like House Majority Leader Kevin McCarthy, of Bakersfield, California, to try to fend off what they view as disruptive enforcement.

"Americans," Hing added, "forget that there is truth to the argument that undocumented immigrants do take jobs Americans don't want to do." The undocumented are also consumers; local economies would suffer if the population vanished suddenly.

Among Trump's favorite campaign stump lines was his vow to build "a great and beautiful wall" that Mexico would be forced to pay for—a vow he's waffled on at times. He also railed against Mexico for "stealing" American jobs because U.S. corporations have factories there. Yet despite his "America first" rhetoric, Trump himself used Mexican and Asian factories to produce his clothing line. The *Washington Post* reported that construction workers on Trump's new hotel in Washington, D.C., admitted just last year that they were undocumented. Trump denied hiring undocumented workers and said the company used E-Verify to conduct screening.

In Florida, the *New York Times* reported that nearly 300 U.S. citizens have applied since 2010 to work as cooks, housekeepers and wait staff at Trump's luxury Mar-a-Lago Club—but that only 17 were hired. The U.S. Labor Department, which reviews whether a business has met requirements to try to hire Americans first, certified 685 H-2B guest worker visas for Mar-a-Lago between 2008 and 2015. CNN reported that over 15 years, Trump's businesses have filed for more than 1,250 foreign workers for various positions. Trump seemed to prefer young, attractive Eastern European or South African people, former workers told CNN.

Trump batted away these findings during the campaign, claiming there were "very few qualified" workers during the "high season" in the Mar-a-Lago area—a claim disputed by services that match employees in the area. Some news reports found that the business did little to meet requirements to advertise for workers. Mar-a-Lago justified its requests for foreign workers by saying that not enough American applicants were willing to work split shifts or part time.

Trump began suggesting in the final days of his campaign he'd go after "criminal" undocumented people first, which is already an Obama administration policy. In a transition video he released to the public on Nov. 21, Trump announced that he plans to direct the U.S. Department of Labor to investigate "all abuses of visa programs that undercut the American worker"—exactly how some in Florida reportedly felt about Trump's recruitment of European guest workers.

"The contradictions with him are enormous," said Muzaffar Chishti, who researches migration and is the director of Migration Policy Institute's office at the New York University School of Law. The Migration Policy Institute is a nonpartisan think tank in Washington, D.C.

When it comes to immigration and accountability, Chishti said, "employers have been able to shift the burden downstream for years now," to subcontractors and workers. Based on Trump's harsh but mercurial rhetoric, Chishti added, it's hard to imagine how Trump's vows to police practices he has reportedly engaged in will eventually play out.

Throughout history, Chishti noted, Americans have employed foreign-born workers, and turned against them in fits of xenophobia that include labeling newcomers as "criminal" or unable to assimilate.

"America's always been ambivalent about immigration," he said, "for a nation of immigrants."

The Aims and Legality of Trump's Executive Orders on Immigration

Jacqueline Varas

Jacqueline Varas is the director of immigration and trade policy at the American Action Forum. Her work has been cited by the Wall Street Journal, *the* Washington Examiner, *CNN, Bloomberg, the Hill, Reuters, and other media outlets.*

Since taking office, President Trump has prioritized restructuring the U.S. immigration system. Within a week of his inauguration, he issued three executive orders that carry significant implications for unauthorized immigrants, legal immigrants, and American taxpayers. The following paper explains each executive order in detail and examines their effects.

Enhancing Public Safety in the Interior of the United States

The first executive order on immigration signed by the president urges the government "to employ all lawful means to enforce the immigration laws of the United States." In accordance with this guidance, the order directs the secretary of homeland security to identify sanctuary cities, i.e. jurisdictions that do not comply with federal enforcement efforts. It also empowers the attorney general to take action against those cities by withholding non-mandatory federal funding.

A jurisdiction can be designated a sanctuary city for a variety of reasons. Local officials may decline to notify U.S. Immigration and Customs Enforcement (ICE) of known unauthorized immigrants, refuse to detain unauthorized immigrants, or refuse to continue detaining unauthorized immigrants past the expiration of their local sentences. Reuters recently found that withholding federal

"An Overview of President Trump's Executive Actions on Immigration," by Jacqueline Varas, American Action Forum, March 13, 2017. Reprinted by permission.

funds from the ten largest sanctuary cities could cost them $2.27 billion in annual grants.

The president's executive order also aims to improve the enforcement of immigration laws related to removable immigrants within the United States. It equally prioritizes the removal of seven categories of immigrants, including those who have been convicted of a crime, been charged with a crime but not yet convicted, and have committed acts that constitute a criminal offense. This includes all unauthorized immigrants who entered the country illegally or overstayed their visas, regardless of whether they have committed a separate crime within the United States. It also applies to lawful immigrants who have committed crimes that qualify them for removal. Accordingly, the president ordered ICE to hire an additional 10,000 enforcement and removal officers, which will triple its size.

President Trump's guidelines will result in stricter enforcement than under the previous administration. In 2015, President Obama changed ICE's enforcement policy by prioritizing the removal of immigrants with felonies or serious misdemeanors and those determined to be a threat to national security. The executive order terminates these priorities and reinstates the Secure Communities Program, which was first put in place in 2008. This program directs local police officers to detain immigrants who are arrested for any offense and found to be removable. However, it was met with backlash after non-criminal unauthorized immigrants with roots in the United States were discovered and removed based on insignificant offenses such as speeding tickets.

This executive order grants more discretionary power to apprehension officers, which has resulted in immigration raids with a stronger focus on non-criminals. However, every immigrant within the United States is entitled to legal counsel and an immigration hearing. President Trump must therefore address the current 540,000 case backlog within the immigration court system in order to successfully carry out his priorities.

Border Security and Immigration Enforcement Improvements

President Trump's second executive order is aimed at enhancing security along the southern border. It orders the construction of a wall between the United States and Mexico to curb unauthorized immigration. By signing this order, President Trump took the first step toward fulfilling one of his biggest campaign promises.

The executive order calls for a wall constructed with "appropriate materials and technology to most effectively achieve complete operational control of the southern border." It also orders the Secretary of Homeland Security to identify all sources of federal funding that can be allocated for construction and to prepare Congressional budget requests. This contradicts Trump's previous statements that Mexico will pay for the wall. However, the president maintains that Mexico will reimburse the United States for all costs.

It is worth noting that Congress already passed legislation authorizing the construction of a physical barrier between the United States and Mexico. The Secure Fence Act, signed by George W. Bush in 2006, called for 700 miles of double-layered fencing along the southern border. At this point, U.S. Customs and Border Protection (CPB) has constructed 654 miles of primary border fencing. However, only 37 miles of secondary fencing and 14 miles of tertiary fencing have been built.

The Department of Homeland Security (DHS) estimated that the president's border wall would cost $21.6 billion and take 3.5 years to construct. President Trump has proposed several methods for obtaining the funds from Mexico: as a candidate, he threatened to halt remittances sent by unauthorized immigrants. These are funds sent from individuals in the United States to their family or friends in Mexico. He also suggested levying tariffs on Mexican imports, imposing visa fees on Mexican immigrants, or cancelling visas to Mexicans altogether.

Most recently, the administration proposed raising funds for the wall through a border-adjustable business cash flow tax, which would replace the current corporate income tax. While this tax reform could raise roughly $12 billion, any new income will likely be used to offset the lost revenue from a lower tax rate on business.

The president's efforts to control unauthorized immigration may be futile if current trends continue. Since the Great Recession, more Mexicans have left the United States than have entered. This may explain why the Mexican unauthorized population has been steadily declining since 2007 and the total unauthorized population has remained stable. Furthermore, almost half of all unauthorized immigrants came to the United States on legal visas. Building a wall will do little to prevent visa overstays.

President Trump's executive action also changes DHS procedure. It orders the detention of all unauthorized immigrants apprehended at the border, including individuals seeking asylum. This differs from previous policy, which allowed apprehended immigrants to be released into the United States and monitored while waiting for an immigration court date or asylum interview. Instead, both Mexican and non-Mexican unauthorized immigrants caught at the border who do not pose a risk of illegal re-entry will be returned to Mexico until a formal removal proceeding can take place.

In FY 2016, almost 60,000 unaccompanied minors were apprehended at the southern border. These individuals are often the children of unauthorized immigrants who are seeking to reunite with their families or escape persecution. A DHS memo on Trump's executive order indicates that family members who helped unaccompanied minors illegally enter the United States may be removed or criminally prosecuted. Finally, the president ordered CPB to hire an additional 5,000 border patrol agents and 500 air & marine agents to enforce these new guidelines.

Protecting the Nation from Foreign Terrorist Entry into the United States

Trump's most controversial executive order introduced a 90 day travel suspension for immigrants from Iraq, Syria, Iran, Libya,

Somalia, Sudan, and Yemen. This order blocked the entry of both immigrants (green card holders) and nonimmigrants (temporary visa holders) into the United States. It was widely perceived to be a Muslim ban, as Trump vowed to impose "a complete shutdown of Muslims entering the United States" during his campaign. However, the president contends that the order does not discriminate on the basis of religion.

The countries singled out by President Trump were first identified by the Obama administration in 2015. After the San Bernardino terrorist attack, President Obama signed a law identifying these nations as countries of concern. This means that individuals who had recently lived in or visited the countries listed could no longer participate in the Visa Waiver Program. While this did not prevent anyone from traveling to the United States, it did prevent them from traveling to the United States without first obtaining a visa.

The purpose of President Trump's executive order was "to ensure that those approved for admission do not intend to harm Americans and that they have no ties to terrorism." However, it faced immediate backlash after legal permanent residents traveling home to the United States were barred from entering the country. The secretary of homeland security subsequently issued a memo excluding lawful permanent residents from the travel suspension.

The travel suspension also resulted in adverse consequences for the United States. For instance, after the U.S. travel ban was put in place, both Iraq and Iran vowed to place reciprocal travel bans on U.S. citizens. This has negative implications for U.S. military and strategic interests in the Middle East. Additionally, the U.S. travel industry lost approximately $185 million in business travel bookings in the week after Trump signed the order.

This executive order also impacts refugees. It suspends all refugee admissions into the United States for 120 days as well as suspends the entrance of Syrian refugees indefinitely. Furthermore, it directs the secretaries of state and homeland security to prioritize the admission of refugees facing religious persecution. This effectively allows the administration to prioritize Christian, Bahá'í, Yazidi or other refugees from the Middle East over others. Finally, it lowers the current limit on refugee entry to the United States from 110,000 per year to 50,000. Over the last ten years, the United States has accepted an average of 62,000 refugees annually.

At least eight groups filed lawsuits alleging that this executive order is unconstitutional. As a result, a U.S. District Judge in Seattle issued a temporary restraining order that halted enforcement of the travel and refugee suspensions nationwide. This restraining order was upheld by the Ninth Circuit Court of Appeals in San Francisco. While the president has the option of taking his case to the Supreme Court, the administrated indicated that it will not appeal the ruling. Instead, President Trump signed a revised executive order that he believes can better withstand legal scrutiny.

Revised: Protecting the Nation from Foreign Terrorist Entry into the United States

The president issued a new travel suspension on Monday that differs from the original in several ways. First, it explicitly excludes green card and other visa holders from the 90-day travel ban. Only individuals applying for new U.S. visas will be affected.

Second, Iraq is no longer included in the temporary travel ban. This comes after concern from the Pentagon and State Department that an Iraqi travel ban would negatively affect joint efforts to fight terrorism. The executive order justifies this change by outlining superior screening measures Iraq has put in place, including "enhance(d) travel documentation, information sharing, and the return of Iraqi nationals subject to final orders of removal." The remaining six countries are still named.

The new order also changes its provisions regarding refugees. Instead of indefinitely barring Syrian refugees from entering the United States, Syrians are now included in the general 120-day refugee suspension. Furthermore, it drops the language prioritizing religious minorities in the refugee program. However, the cap on refugee entry is still lowered to 50,000 per year.

To avoid confusion at U.S. ports of entry, the president's revised order does not go into effect until March 16th. This gives local officials ten days to fully understand its provisions and whom they apply to. It also provides time for officers to prepare and coordinate their enforcement efforts.

The president defended his executive order by declaring "the U.S. government must ensure that those entering this country will not harm the American people ... (and) do not bear malicious intent toward the United States." However, DHS concluded last month that "country of citizenship is unlikely to be a reliable indicator of potential terrorist activity."

Not surprisingly, the new travel suspension is just as controversial as the first: seven states have already joined a lawsuit against it. It remains to be seen whether the president's revised executive order will hold up in court.

Travel Ban Would Compel Muslim Countries to Address Internal Problems

Salim Mansur

Salim Mansur is an associate professor of political science at the University of Western Ontario in Canada and a distinguished senior fellow at the Gatestone Institute

- Trump's call to ban the entry of Muslims to the U.S. seemed to indicate that it should be temporary, until the American leadership has figured out what in the complex reality of the Muslim world—religious, political, economic, cultural, and so on—contributes to turning a significant portion of Muslims into jihadi operatives at war with the United States.

- Despite numerous terrorist attacks carried out by extremist Muslims inside the United States, Americans have *not* turned against their Muslim neighbors; on the contrary, Americans and Europeans in general have continued to be accommodating, tolerant, even protective, of Muslims in their midst, in keeping with their secular and liberal democratic values.

- Americans have watched the unabated spread of terrorism and warfare in the name of Islam; the intensity of hatred in Muslim countries directed towards the United States; the attacks on Americans by extremist Muslims; and the betrayals by Muslim countries that have been receiving American assistance, such as Pakistan.

- The elite in Muslim-majority states is mostly, if not entirely, responsible for the wretched state of affairs that has left those states at the bottom of the list of countries when measured in terms of economic development, human rights, gender equality, education, freedom and democracy.

"Trump's Ban on Muslims: The Discussion the Media Won't Have," by Salim Mansur, Gatestone Institute, February 6, 2016. Reprinted by permission.

- For the elite in third world societies, a getaway to America has meant a readily available exit to avoid being held accountable for their misdeeds.
- Herein lies the irony of a Trump's proposed ban: it would greatly affect the Muslim elite and, consequently, compel them to begin taking responsibility for how they have mismanaged their societies and impoverished their people.

On December 7, 2015, U.S. presidential candidate Donald Trump's campaign released a press statement calling "for a complete and total shutdown of Muslims entering the United States until our representatives can figure out what is going on." He was publicly saying what an increasing number of Americans over the years have apparently begun to think about Muslims and Islam in terms of the "clear and present" danger to their security and their country.

A press release explained the reason for the ban:

"Without looking at the various polling data, it is obvious to anybody the hatred is beyond comprehension. Where this hatred comes from and why we will have to determine. Until we are able to determine and understand this problem and the dangerous threat it poses, our country cannot be the victims (sic) of horrendous attacks by people that believe only in Jihad, and have no sense of reason or respect for human life."

Immediately there was a chorus of denunciation of Trump by his political opponents—both Democrats and Republicans—as well as the White House. Support for Trump among Republican primary voters, however, spiked upwards.

A few days before Trump made his call for banning Muslims, the Former Prime Minister of Britain, Tony Blair, described the extent to which ISIS, or Daesh, unless defeated, poses a serious security threat to the West. ISIS-controlled territory in Iraq and Syria is now as large as the United Kingdom; its influence reaches far beyond, into North and sub-Saharan Africa, Egypt, the Gaza Strip, and even Southeast Asia.

Blair stated—after the ritual statement, that

"Islam, as practiced and understood by the large majority of believers, is a peaceful and honourable faith. ... a large majority of Muslims completely reject Daesh-like Jihadism and the terrorism which comes with it."

"However, in many Muslim countries large numbers also believe that the CIA or Jews were behind 9/11. Clerics who proclaim that non-believers and apostates must be killed or call for Jihad against Jews have twitter followings running into millions."

Despite the reality that Blair described, there still remains much reluctance among politicians in the West to speak frankly about the deep-seated problems of the Muslim world, especially in North Africa and the Middle East. These problems have made violence endemic, and the living conditions of most people in terror-affected regions unbearable. This politically correct reluctance to hold the Muslims who commit violence accountable for the threats they pose to others has become, over time, untenable.

Superficially, political correctness seems like a kind-hearted civility towards others and empathy with the less fortunate. At a deeper level, however it represents a self-serving uneasiness at possibly being thought judgmental or branded as bigot. At the very deepest level, it is an insult: it infantilizes a vast group of people, as one assumed they were mentally or emotionally incompetent, incapable of take responsibility for their own lives by themselves. In politics, just as self-serving, the reluctance to speak up doubtless springs from the fear of not snagging every possible vote.

Since 9/11, Americans have grown increasingly curious about Muslims and Islam. They seem to have wanted to learn about the culture, politics and history of the Muslim world. The same cannot be said about Muslims. They do not seem to want to acquire a deeper understanding about America and the West.

There also seems to be a disconnect between Americans in general, and the reflexively politically correct establishment, along with the mainstream media. As Americans watched, President

Obama and his administration have engaged in euphemisms to speak about Muslim terrorists or Islamic extremism. Instead, they are referred to as "man-caused disasters" or "workplace violence," while the "global war on terror" was replaced by "overseas contingency operations."

The coddling of Muslims and Islam, the fear of giving offense that might fuel more Muslim violence, became the hallmark of the Obama Administration. Even as the situation in the Middle East and the surrounding region radically worsened, the Obama Administration adopted a policy of appeasing Muslims instead of challenging or confronting them.

Trump not only exploited this disconnect to his advantage, but also indicated his intention to reassess America's relationship with the Muslim world. An examination of the West's partnership with the Middle East is much needed. "It is where," in Blair's words, "the heart of Islam beats."

ii.

It is important to note that Trump's call is not directed at Islam, but at Muslims—a subtle yet important distinction that got obscured in the controversy on the subject. The ban is, after all, conditional—until the American people and their government have figured out what in the complex reality of the Muslim world—religious, political, economic and cultural—contributes to turning a significant portion of Muslims into jihadi operatives at war against the United States (especially those from the Middle East, North Africa and Southwest Asia).

In making the distinction between Muslims and Islam—the people, not the religion—Trump avoided getting into the weeds of theological debates on Islam. Islam, to many of its critics, is seen as the source of the problem: less of as a religion and more of as a totalitarian ideology.

It is doubtful, however, if such debates have any meaning for the roughly 1.7 billion Muslims, whose numbers are steadily increasing, in terms of undermining their belief in Islam. Such debates mocking what they hold sacred only mock what they hold sacred, and provoke that segment of the Muslim population readily given to rage and violence.

However, a message is being sent: that unless many Muslims can change demonstrably to accept and abide by the social and political norms of American democracy, they may be excluded from entering the United States as immigrants.

This message goes beyond the immediate concerns about vetting for security purposes the Syrian refugees fleeing the devastations of the civil war in their countries: It raises the stakes for Muslims wishing to emigrate to the United States.

This view, if you think about it, is not outrageous. It is, and should be, the right of a nation to insist on the sovereignty of its borders and to decide who may or may not enter the country. Indeed, in accordance with the existing U.S. laws, the President is constitutionally empowered under Title 8 (Aliens and Nationality) of the U.S. Code, section 1182, to decide who is inadmissible into the country. It is likely, however, that eventually the higher courts may have to decide.

In the meantime, the Muslim world has been put on notice that immigrating to the United States it may no longer be "business as usual" for everyone. Rather, the statement should probably be seen as a warning that the time might have come for Muslims and their governments to examine their share of responsibility in the making of such a ban on Muslims entering America.

iii.

The threats from, and the carnage brought about by, extremist Muslims bent upon pushing their global Jihad continue, more or less unchecked. While the emergence of ISIS has destabilized the Middle East and the surrounding region, the specter of radical Islam now hangs ominously over Europe. Tony Blair also said:

> "The impact of terrorism is never simply about the tragedy of lives lost. It is the sense of instability, insecurity and fear that comes in its wake...And in the case of nations like ours,

with our proud and noble traditions of tolerance and liberty, it makes those very strengths seem like weaknesses in the face of an onslaught that cares nothing for our values and hates our way of life."

Since the attacks of 9/11/2001, Americans have watched how Western democracies have been overly sensitive in *not* smearing or profiling all Muslims in countering the violence and terror of the extremist Muslims in their midst. Americans accepted with little protest the extent to which their open and free lifestyle was altered due to security concerns after those attacks. Since then, despite terrorist attacks carried out by extremist Muslims inside the United States, Americans did *not* turn against their Muslim neighbors. On the contrary, Americans and Europeans, in keeping with their secular and liberal democratic values, have continued to be incredibly accommodating, tolerant, and even protective of the Muslims in their midst.

Americans have also watched the broadening spread of terrorism and warfare in the name of Islam; the intensity of hatred in Muslim countries directed towards the United States; the attacks on American missions; the kidnapping and murder of American citizens by extremist Muslims; and the double-dealing and betrayal by Muslim countries receiving American assistance, such as Pakistan.

They have watched the physical destruction in the Middle East of Christian communities among the oldest in the world; the massacre of Yezidis and other minorities in Syria and Iraq; and the attacks on Coptic Christians of Egypt whose presence in the Nile valley pre-dates the arrival of Arabs as Muslims in the seventh century, C.E.

Americans have watched the unremitting violence of Palestinians against Jews in Israel, and have heard—and keep hearing—the bile of anti-Semitic racism flood forth from the mouths of political leaders, such as former President Mahmoud Ahmadinejad of Iran and former Prime Minister Mahathir Mohamad of Malaysia, from mosque pulpits across the Muslim world, from sanctimonious Europeans and from the viciously bigoted United Nations.

All the while, Americans have waited to hear Muslims in their midst—safe and secure from the savagery across the Middle East and North Africa—step forward in credible numbers to condemn the perpetrators of such horrific violence. Often they are happy to denounce "violence," but almost never by naming names. The failure to do so raises suspicions—not surprisingly—that maybe most Muslims are in favor of such actions.

Meaningful condemnations, to be taken seriously by non-Muslims, could then become the prelude to repudiating those interpretations of Islam that provide for the incitement and justification of violence through jihad.

If Americans, and others in the West, heard Muslims in America more or less unanimously denounce jihadi violence and repudiate the interpretations of Islam that call for warfare against non-Muslims as infidels, this would be doubly reassuring. There would be the promise that American Muslims—secure in their new world home and secure in their faith protected in America—have the confidence, like Egypt's Abdel Fattah al-Sisi, to call for reforming Islam, as well as reconciling their belief with modern science and democracy. Americans could see that that Muslims in America are loyal Americans, pledged to defend, protect, and abide by the American constitution.

Instead, organizations claiming to represent American Muslims, such as the Council of American-Islamic Relations (CAIR) and Islamic Society of North America (ISNA), and many local imams or religious leaders in mosques across America, continually appear in media defending Muslims as victims of anti-Islamic bigotry or explaining away Muslim violence and terror as misguided and nothing to do with the "true" teachings of Islam—when neither could be farther from the truth.

Moreover, these organizations are publicly committed to the demand that the American government and courts allow Muslims in America to live in accordance with the code of Islamic laws, Sharia. Again, Americans have not heard from a sufficient number of Muslims who reject such divisive and regressive demands pushed by CAIR or ISNA in their name.

CAIR, ISNA, and other similar Muslim organizations—either based in mosques, or organized with the support of mosques and offshore money from oil-rich Middle Eastern countries—have their origin in the ideology and politics of the Muslim Brotherhood (MB), founded in Egypt in the 1920s by Hassan al-Banna. His theological innovation was to turn the idea of jihad, or holy war, against non-believers into the organizing principle of his movement. Jihad would reconstitute post-colonial Muslim societies, such as Egypt, on the basis of Sharia and re-establish the institution of the Caliphate abolished by Mustafa Kemal [Ataturk] of Turkey when the Ottoman Empire was dismantled after World War I.

In recent months, beginning with Egypt under President Abdel Fattah el-Sisi, Arab member-states of the Gulf Co-operation Council (GCC)—led by the United Arab Emirates (UAE) and supported by Saudi Arabia—declared the Muslim Brotherhood to be a terrorist organization in collusion with ISIS. This conclusion apparently has not registered with CAIR and ISNA in America. There has been no sign of American Muslims stepping forth in appreciably large numbers to denounce the Muslim Brotherhood as a terrorist organization and dissociate themselves from the Muslim Brotherhood and all Muslim organizations with links to it.

Americans, driven by their own, have learned since 9/11 that although all Muslims are not terrorists, most terrorists in the news turn out to be Muslims. They have also observed that there is a sufficiently large segment of Muslims sympathetic to whichever cause these terrorists espouse in their attempts to justify their violence. Americans have similarly learned that while Islam is a world religion with a rich and complex history, there is also an aspect in Islam—although it is not unique to Islam—that sanctions violence against non-believers—both as a defensive measure and to spread Islam beyond its traditional frontiers.

When Trump announced that he would ban Muslims entering America until the representatives of American people have figured out why Muslims hate America, he was speaking for a large number of Americans, even perhaps a majority.

The failing of Muslims in America to take a clear stand against terrorism; and against the parts of Islamic theology that incites and justifies violence against non-believers in Islam. Sadly, Jew-hatred and anti-Christian bigotry have become the signature of Muslim extremists and have contributed to the rising suspicion among Americans that many Muslims are disloyal to America after making it their home.

iv.

Any ban on Muslims entering America would hurt most severely the upper fifth segment of Muslims in their countries. This segment of the Muslim population forms the elite, and this elite is mostly, if not entirely, responsible for the wretched state of affairs that has left the Muslim majority states languishing at the bottom of the list of countries terms of economic development, human rights, gender equality, education, freedom, democracy, or any other criterion.

Immigrating to America became for Muslims belonging to the elite segment of their societies the pathway to escape the anger and frustration of the people as their living conditions worsened. In third world societies, a get-away to America has meant for the elite a readily available exit to avoid being held accountable for their misdeeds.

Herein lies the irony of a U.S. ban: those it would affect most are the Muslim elite, and it would consequently compel them to begin taking responsibility for how they have mismanaged their societies and impoverished their people.

A U.S. ban would set the precedent for other Western democracies to follow, and thereby instill a positive external pressure for the reform from inside Islam and Muslim societies, and greatly assist the efforts of the many Muslims working to reform Islam.

Positive changes in repressive societies could take place the same way as after the signing of the human rights section of the 1975 Helsinki Accords. The Helsinki Accords provided indispensable support from the outside to human rights activists as well as to dissidents inside the communist states of Eastern Europe.

Eventually the pressure on the Soviet Union and its East European allies to abide by the human rights section of the Accords they had signed dramatically accelerated the end of the Cold War and the disintegration of the Soviet Union. "Rarely," Henry Kissinger wrote in *Years of Renewal*, "has a diplomatic process so illuminated the limitations of human foresight."

Until now, there has been no coordinated effort by Western democracies to put pressure on Muslim countries to abide by the principles of the Universal Declaration of Human Rights (UDHR) to which they, as member-states of the United Nations, are signatories. Instead, Western democracies have continued to accommodate Muslim states even as their governments failed to abide by the UDHR, violated human rights of their people, made war, engaged in genocide, and raised and armed terrorists who spread terror by attacking non-Muslim states.

In his final State of the Union address to the American people on January 12, 2016, President Barack Obama spoke about how his administration is engaged in containing, degrading, and defeating "terrorist networks." What he did not mention were the repeated atrocities committed by Muslim terrorists within the United States, the most recent of which, under his watch, being the massacre in San Bernardino. He did not express the outrage most Americans must have felt watching the attacks on Christian communities of the Middle East, the killing of Christians and minorities by ISIS, the destruction of churches, ancient sites, and works of art from pre-Islamic times in the region. He also did not acknowledge the revulsion Americans must have felt seeing videos of people drowned or burned alive, or having their throats slit by ISIS. These atrocities do not even include ISIS buying and selling kidnapped women and children from minority communities as sex slave—and all (accurately) in the name of unreformed Islam.

Instead, President Obama said:

> "[W]e need to reject any politics—any politics—that targets people because of race or religion. Let me just say this. This is not a matter of political correctness. This is a matter of understanding just what it is that makes us strong...When politicians insult Muslims, whether abroad or our fellow citizens, when a mosque is vandalized, or a kid is called names, that doesn't make us safer. That's not telling it like it is. It's just wrong. It diminishes us in the eyes of the world."

Obama was engaged in coddling Muslims in the mistaken belief that displaying respect for, and muting criticism of, their faith and them would help to repair the broken friendship between America and the world of Muslims. This was the same message Obama had taken to Cairo, Egypt, soon after his inauguration in 2009, seemingly trying to demonstrate through public diplomacy his own understanding of Islam that his presidency would write a new and better chapter of American-Muslim relations.

But this promise of healing America's relationship with the Muslim world now, in the eighth and final year of Obama's term as president, has not materialized. For this failure, Americans cannot be faulted. On the contrary, Americans have watched the situation within the Middle East and the surrounding region dramatically worsen, and the malady of failed Muslim states, with the problems Muslim refugees brought with them to Europe, be exported to the West.

This is why Americans in general—unlike their own elite in politics, business, the media or academia—have not been outraged by calls to ban Muslims from entering the United States. Trump has expressed publicly what many Americans might privately be thinking would be a circumspect thing to do—as Trump stated, until Americans have figured out what makes many Muslims hate America with such an intensity that they turn to violence and murder.

Until then, a ban on immigration might at last compel Muslims to examine their own ills and start working to remedy them. This certainly—both for Muslims and non-Muslims—could be only for the good.

Reports Emerge of US Customs and Border Patrol Abuses

Alice Miranda Ollstein

Alice Miranda Ollstein is a reporter covering Congress, the Supreme Court, and the White House for Talking Points Memo. She has also worked for outlets like ThinkProgress and Free Speech Radio News.

Amid the chaos and heartache caused by President Donald Trump's executive order blocking immigrants and refugees from seven majority-Muslim nations, stories have emerged of U.S. Customs and Border Patrol (CBP) agents pressuring visa holders to sign away their rights and exit the country.

When Trump unveiled the executive order, he said it would ensure "extreme vetting" of immigrants and refugees from Iran, Iraq, Libya, Somalia, Sudan, Syria, and Yemen. There is nothing in the text of the order about an I-407 form—the document that immigrants sign when they want to renounce their U.S. residency, waive their right to a hearing with an immigration judge, and leave the country. Yet the *New York Times, L.A. Times,* the Spanish-language news wire EFE, and other news outlets are reporting accusations that CBP officers are inappropriately pressuring visa holders from the seven banned countries to sign that form upon arrival.

ThinkProgress has learned that citizens of nations *not* listed in the executive order are being targeted, as well.

Immigrants, attorneys, Mexican government officials, and U.S. lawmakers are accusing CBP of coercing legal permanent residents (green card holders) and visa holders into renouncing their visas and leaving the country, without giving them a full explanation of the repercussions.

"Customs Agents Accused of Targeting People from Nations Not in Trump's Travel Ban," by Alice Miranda Ollstein, ThinkProgress, February 15, 2017. Reprinted by permission.

Hustled onto a Flight Home

The same week the executive order was signed, a 37-year-old industrial engineer arrived in Houston, where she had a layover on her way to attending her cousin's 30th birthday party in Los Angeles.

The woman, who ThinkProgress will identify as Jeni after she requested anonymity because she is involved in ongoing legal proceedings, was born and raised in Juarez, Mexico, right on the border with the United States. Jeni said she has been traveling to the U.S. with a visitor's visa since her childhood. In dozens of trips over three decades, she told ThinkProgress in a phone interview, she never had Customs agents do more than check her suitcase and ask her a few questions. This time, however, agents brought her into a separate room, where they questioned her for hours about her family, work history, and previous visits. She said they patted her down, fingerprinted her, and photographed her.

Jeni said agents accused her of overstaying her visa on a trip nine years ago, which she denied. They then accused her of working without permission on her last U.S. visit, when she volunteered for the Odiyan Center, a Buddhist retreat center in California.

The Odiyan Center confirmed to ThinkProgress that Jeni had volunteered there in 2016 and had not worked for pay. While it is illegal for immigrants like Jeni with a B1/B2 visitor's visa to do any work—paid or unpaid—that benefits a commercial enterprise, the Buddhist center does not qualify as such. The visa does allow holders to volunteer for "a recognized religious or nonprofit charitable organization."

After the interview, Jeni said the CPB officers handed her a stack of forms and told her: "Hurry up. Your flight is leaving. We're going to send you back to Mexico. If you don't sign, you will go to a detention center until we can find another flight for you, and we don't know when that will be."

Jeni said the agents did not explain to her what the forms meant and did not inform her of her right to consult with a lawyer. When she reviewed the documents later, she discovered she had forfeited her visa and is now banned from returning to the United States for the next five years. She will not be able to visit her family members in Los Angeles, and she fears the ban will hurt her future career prospects.

"I'm an industrial engineer, and most manufacturing companies are international," she explained. "At past jobs, they have asked us to go do trainings in the United States. I obviously now won't be able to do it, and maybe that will be an obstacle for me getting a job."

Jeni said she will continue talking to lawyers and the Mexican consulate in El Paso, Texas, about her options for challenging the travel ban, but she is not optimistic about her prospects. She observed that if she was so readily misled into signing away her rights—despite being fluent in English and a frequent traveler—then CBP may be taking advantage of many other travelers who might be more easily confused.

"I've had a visa since I was a kid. It's not like I don't know the process," she said. "I've never done anything unlawful, but here I am."

The I-407 Form: A Troubling Pattern Emerges

Accounts from members of Congress, immigration attorneys, and the Mexican government confirm that Jeni's story is not an isolated incident.

"They're deliberately misleading people," said a Mexican government official about CBP agents. The official, familiar with consular affairs, spoke with ThinkProgress on the condition of anonymity, citing the current sensitivity of U.S.-Mexican relations. "They are offering an option that shouldn't even be on the table."

Official CBP policy dictates that an I-407 form should only be offered if the visa holder has spent more than a year outside the United States, has failed to file income taxes, or has committed a crime serious enough to warrant deportation. Additionally, the Inspector's Field Manual for Customs and Border Protection reads: "The inspecting officer must never coax or coerce an alien to surrender his or her alien registration document in lieu of a removal hearing."

Yet the Mexican government official said he has received reports of Mexican visa holders who were handed the I-407 form at airports and told, "You should do this."

"The way it was told to us by those who encountered it," the official said, "was that they said: 'Here's this paper, and if you don't do this, there will be some sort of backlash.'"

The official noted that Mexico has more direct traffic with the United States than any other nation, so any slight policy change will invariably impact their citizens. But he also wonders if Mexicans are being singled as a result of the increasingly hostile political environment. With a commander-in-chief known for calling Mexicans criminals, rapists, and "bad hombres," federal officials on the ground may feel empowered to discriminate.

"This enables others in government or just average U.S. citizens to keep treating Mexicans in a negative way," he said. "And it seems some people in the position to do so are taking advantage of the atmosphere created by the executive order and the confusion that has reigned in some places in the country."

Mexico is not the only nation impacted. Vivian Khalaf, an attorney with the Arab American Bar Association in Chicago, told ThinkProgress that CBP agents handed the form to a Jordanian client of hers when he arrived at O'Hare Airport in late January, and instructed him to sign it, despite the fact that he did not meet any of the criteria.

"He was only outside the U.S. for 10 months, but they questioned him for over an hour about why he spent so much time out of the country," she said. "The CBP officer then told him that he doesn't need a green card if he doesn't intend to live here." Khalaf had warned him before traveling not to sign anything at the airport, and the client declined to sign the form.

Not only is Jordan *not* on the list of countries that Trump singled out for "extreme vetting," Khalaf told ThinkProgress that in 27 years of practicing law, she had never heard of agents pushing the I-407 form on anyone from any country who had been abroad for less than a year.

Marcelino Miranda at the Mexican Consulate in Chicago told ThinkProgress that while his regional office has received no reports of this happening since the executive order, they are putting out messages on social media "advising people to be vigilant."

"We are warning people not to sign any documents and telling them that they have the right to call a lawyer or the consulate," Miranda said. "And we tell people to report any case where they feel their rights are being abused or they are forced to sign something they don't understand."

Questions Remain About Undue Pressure on Migrants

CBP did not respond to ThinkProgress' questions about the allegations of coercion, the number of visa holders who have been given I-407 forms since Trump's executive order, and whether their policies regarding the forms have changed.

The agency has similarly stonewalled members of Congress who wrote to CBP in early February demanding answers to these same questions, citing reports from their constituents of "coercion and egregious violations of basic due process" at Los Angeles International Airport (LAX).

"Applications of form I-407 appear to have been carried out in an abusive and illegal manner," the representatives wrote, describing an instance in which an Iranian green card holder was coerced by CBP officials at LAX into signing the form and boarding a plane back to Iran.

"The response from CBP was absolutely horrendous," said Rep. Judy Chu (D-CA) who went to LAX the day the executive order took effect and drafted the letter to CBP. "When we demanded to see CBP and get an accounting of what was going on, they said to call the Public Information Office. But when we did, nobody answered the phone. It was a dead end. So we called the Commander back, and she actually hung up on us. And we are members of Congress."

More than a dozen other California Democrats then joined Chu in demanding CBP review all I-407 forms signed since the executive order took effect and report back to them on any documented cases of coercion.

"It just shows that this executive order is so sloppily executed and chaotic," she said. "It created mass confusion and injustice on the ground. They're threatening these very desperate individuals with indefinite detention until they get a court hearing. So they think, 'Oh I'll just sign this instead.' A person could easily find themselves being deported through a supposedly voluntary process. In reality, it's not voluntary at all."

The Letter of the Law

Even for travelers from the seven countries outlined in the executive order, CBP's use of the I-407 form may violate federal law. Sixty people from those countries sued President Trump and CBP in a Virginia federal court a few days after the ban went into effect, alleging that agents engaged in an "illegal scheme to mislead and pressure visa holders into signing away their rights."

"Department of Homeland Security officials have been effectuating the ban by bullying these arriving immigrants into 'voluntarily' relinquishing their claims to lawful permanent residence into the United States," the lawsuit reads. "They made neither a free choice nor an informed choice."

The lead plaintiffs in the suit are two Yemeni brothers, Tareq Aqel Mohammed Aziz and Ammar Aqel Mohammed Aziz, who arrived on immediate relative immigrant visas on January 28 to reunite with their father, a U.S. citizen. The executive order went into effect while they were in the air.

"This was a moment that they and their father had waited for and dreamed of for many years," the lawsuit said. "But their dream quickly and inexplicably converted into a nightmare: instead of being permitted to transit to their connecting flight, Tareq and Ammar were handcuffed, detained, forced to sign papers that they neither read nor understood, and then placed onto a return flight to Ethiopia just two and a half hours after their landing."

The lawsuit accuses CBP of violating the travelers' constitutional right to due process and equal protection under the law by "coercing the relinquishment of rights" and lying to immigrants about the consequences of the I-407 form.

"An employee or agent of respondents falsely informed Tareq and Ammar that, if they did not sign the documents, they would be sent to Yemen and that they would be barred from returning to the United States for five years," the suit claims.

Attorneys for the 60 deported individuals estimate that "dozens if not hundreds" have been similarly coerced into signing the forms in airports around the country, and say the illegal practice even continued after a federal judge issued a temporary restraining order.

Government officials and attorneys say the improper use of the forms is happening not only at airports but at U.S. border crossings—where tens of thousands of visa and green card holders enter every day.

"I was told that some immigration officers took away green cards. I checked with some colleagues and it seemed there were some people at the border," said consular official Miranda. "But it was just a tiny, few number of cases out of all the thousands of people crossing the border."

El Paso immigration attorney Melissa Lopez has also heard reports from reliable sources who regularly work with immigrants in El Paso.

"The first weekend after the executive order, on the bridge [between Juarez, Mexico and El Paso, Texas], two or three people were basically forced into signing the I-407 form, and made to feel that they had no choice," she said. "Honestly, in the nine and a half years I've been doing this, I can't ever remember hearing of this ever happening at a port of entry."

Lopez, who works with the faith-based human rights group Diocesan Migrant and Refugee Services, stressed that she hasn't been able to track down the people targeted by this practice to verify the claims. She assumes they are afraid to come forward and speak out about their legal situation.

Still, she is warning her clients and the broader immigrant community not to sign anything at the border crossing and to insist on seeing an immigration judge. Only a judge, not a CBP officer, she said, can determine whether someone has done something serious enough to warrant losing their residency. But what bothers Lopez is that CBP is not being up front about how they are interpreting the president's new policy.

"The most concerning thing was that the executive order was only supposed to be focused on seven countries but we saw it affect Mexicans, who weren't supposed to be included at all," she said. "It very much seems like the executive order made some officers feel emboldened to treat people differently and make them feel they don't have rights. It became an excuse for them to pursue improper actions against people, and gave them a free card to do whatever they wanted."

Chu and her colleagues in Congress say they will continue to press the Department of Homeland Security for answers.

"We want to know what is actually in the directive given to Border Patrol personnel," she told ThinkProgress. "We want to know how the executive order is being interpreted. Most importantly, we want to know how many I-407s were signed after the executive order and how many actually resulted in people deporting themselves. We want to know whether the acts of coercion are being stopped by the federal judge's order that stopped the whole thing and whether the forms people did sign will be invalidated."

Most Deportees Are Not Violent Criminals

Teresa Wiltz

Teresa Wiltz is a veteran journalist who covers demographics for the Pew Charitable Trust's Stateline blog.

L ast December, Mayra Machado was pulled over for a routine traffic stop in Arkansas. Turns out she had an unpaid ticket for failing to yield. And as a teen, she'd spent four months in boot camp for writing bad checks. Now 31, the single mother of three, who is an undocumented immigrant, faces imminent deportation to El Salvador, the battle-scarred country she fled when she was 5 years old.

Sylvester Owino, 40, said he survived torture in Kenya as a young activist and came to the U.S. on a student visa, which ran out. A 2003 robbery conviction in San Diego resulted in a nine-year stint in a detention facility. Now, he is part of a U.S. Supreme Court case that will determine whether immigrant detainees have a right to a bond hearing.

The two situations illustrate the variety of crimes that can get immigrants detained and deported, even after they have served a jail or prison sentence for the crime—and even if they are in the country legally. And while the federal government says it targets noncitizens who are serious or repeat offenders, immigrants with minor offenses often are deported.

Immigrants with criminal records may soon come under increased scrutiny. Republican President-elect Donald Trump has pledged to immediately deport "the people that are criminal and have criminal records." There are, he said, "a lot of these people, probably two million, it could be even three million, we are getting them out of our country."

"What Crimes Are Eligible for Deportation?" by Teresa Wiltz, the Pew Charitable Trusts, December 21, 2016. Reprinted by permission. © The Pew Charitable Trusts.

Immigration advocates say those numbers are inflated and point to figures that indicate most immigrants are being deported for minor crimes or for no crime at all.

First-generation immigrants commit crimes at much lower rates than do U.S. citizens. But for those who do commit crimes, it's hard to get a clear picture of whether they are serious or misdemeanors, violent or nonviolent.

Since 2014, the Department of Homeland Security has prioritized deporting noncitizens who pose a serious threat to public safety or national security—and from October 2014 through September 2015, of the 235,413 people who were deported, 59 percent had criminal convictions.

But federal data on criminal deportees does not specify the crimes they've committed—or how many of them are undocumented. Technically, if someone is undocumented and entered the country after January 2014, they are considered a high priority for criminal deportation, even if they have committed no other offense.

Further complicating matters: what constitutes a "criminal alien" is not defined in U.S. immigration law or regulations and is used broadly, according to a September report by the Congressional Research Service. A criminal alien may be someone who is undocumented or an authorized immigrant who may or may not be deportable, depending on the crime they have committed. He or she may be incarcerated or free, or have already served time.

"We see a ton of people deported for misdemeanors, probation violations, petty theft, shoplifting," said Alisa Wellek, executive director of the Immigrant Defense Project, a legal services group that advocates for immigrant rights in the criminal justice system.

"The federal government has these really overreaching laws on the books, laws that are very unforgiving for anyone who's had any contact with the criminal justice system—even if you've never served a day in jail."

Noncitizens convicted of an "aggravated felony" face particularly harsh penalties. Congress expanded the definition of the term since 1988 so that they can be deported for a crime that may be neither "aggravated" nor a "felony," according to Joshua Breisblatt, policy analyst for the American Immigration Council, a pro-immigration research group.

Thirty offenses qualify as aggravated felonies, including theft, failing to appear in court, or offenses that most states consider a misdemeanor or do not criminalize at all, such as consensual sex between a 21-year-old and a 17-year-old, the group said.

Any new offense Congress adds to the list is retroactive. So a noncitizen can become deportable even if he or she already served the sentence for the crime years before.

When she was 19, Machado pleaded guilty to three felony counts: forging a friend's name on a check, writing bad checks, and failing to appear in court.

Because of her criminal history, Machado is considered a "priority aggravated felon," according to a U.S. Immigration and Customs Enforcement (ICE) official.

Machado, who considers herself "totally Americanized," is in a detention facility in Louisiana. She is facing deportation any day now to El Salvador, a country where she said she knows no one and cannot read or write the language.

Targeted for Deportation

In 2014, President Barack Obama announced stepped-up deportation for "felons, not families." At the same time, the Department of Homeland Security announced that it would be prioritizing deporting noncitizens who posed a serious threat to public safety or national security.

Research by immigration think tanks indicates that serious crimes committed by noncitizens are rare. The Migration Policy Institute estimates that of the roughly 1.9 million noncitizens who are eligible for deportation based on their criminal history, about 820,000 are undocumented. Of those, 37 percent, or roughly

300,000, were convicted of a felony, which can range from murder to attempting to re-enter the country illegally, said Faye Hipsman, an MPI policy analyst.

Another 47 percent, or about 390,000, were convicted of a significant misdemeanor, such as drunken driving. But what constitutes a misdemeanor can vary greatly from state to state, and can be anything from shoplifting to minor drug possession, Hipsman said, and sometimes people with low-level traffic violations get caught up in the deportation pipeline.

But ICE says about 85 percent of people in detention facilities are there because they were considered "top priority" for removal— either they were a threat to public safety or national security, or they were attempting to cross the border illegally, or they were members of a criminal gang, or they had been convicted of a felony, or they were considered "aggravated felons."

Advocates for limiting immigration, such as Jessica Vaughan of the Center for Immigration Studies, urge the incoming Trump administration to get tougher and scrap the practice of ranking crimes to decide who should be deported.

The policy, she said, "exempted too many criminal aliens from deportation and allowed for exemptions based on family ties." "All of that resulted in the release of tens of thousands of criminal aliens in the past few years," Vaughan said. "Many of these individuals went on to commit more crimes, sometimes with tragic results."

Many local law enforcement officials agree, although many of them ignore ICE requests to detain people without a court order for fear they could be found in violation of immigrants' civil rights.

The sheriff of Rockland County, Texas, Harold Eavenson, said he has seen more than his share of immigrants committing crimes, including a hit-and-run homicide committed by a man who'd been deported and then came back.

"There should be no doubt at all that anyone who has a criminal history in this country should be deported," said Eavenson, who is slated to become president of the National Sheriffs' Association in 2017. "I've seen illegals who have been deported seven or eight times," he said. "The reason they keep coming back is they know there are no consequences."

A Closer Look

One way to get a glimpse into the types of crimes immigrants have been convicted of is to look at so-called detainers. Detainers are requests by ICE to local, state and federal law enforcement to hold noncitizens for possible deportation.

Half of the 95,085 immigrants targeted by ICE for possible criminal deportation in fiscal 2015 did not have criminal convictions at all, according to an analysis of ICE data by the Transactional Records Access Clearinghouse at Syracuse University. (TRAC has examined detainer requests issued between 2003 and 2015, which it obtained through the Freedom of Information Act.)

The rest had convictions for drunken driving (6.7 percent), assault (4 percent), drug trafficking (2.1 percent), burglary (1.8 percent), sale of marijuana (1.7 percent) and traffic offense (1.6 percent). Fewer still had convictions for illegal entry, larceny, sale of cocaine and domestic violence.

All the evidence shows that serious crimes committed by noncitizens are "extremely rare," said TRAC Director Susan Long. "The issue is, what do you do when you can't find that many serious criminals?" she said. "We don't want murderers and rapists in our midst regardless of their citizenship, but you have to find them."

A detainer is the first step in a long process and does not always include complete details of a detainee's criminal history, according to ICE officials.

Mass Incarceration and Black Immigrants

Black immigrants are particularly susceptible to getting caught in the prison-deportation pipeline, said Wellek of the Immigrant Defense Project.

According a 2016 report by the Black Alliance for Just Immigration, a research and advocacy group, more than one in five noncitizens facing deportation for criminal offenses is black. Black immigrants also are more likely than other immigrants to be deported because of a conviction.

Back home in Kenya, Owino was a track star, representing his country in international competitions. He was well-known—and he was outspoken about police corruption and human rights violations, he said, and that made him a target of police. After he was arrested and tortured twice, Owino said, he applied for a student visa and started attending college in San Diego in 1998.

But 18 months shy of graduation, he said, the combination of alcohol and gambling, plus the breakup of his marriage and "bad memories" from his life in Kenya sent him into a downward spiral. Owino dropped out of school and ended up living in the streets—and overstaying his visa. He said he was hungry and desperate when he decided to rob a beauty salon. "I forced myself and demanded money," Owino said. "I was super drunk. Police caught me two blocks away."

No one was hurt, but because Owino brandished a penknife during the course of the robbery, he was sentenced to three years in state prison. After serving most of his term, Owino was transferred to a detention facility, where he waited for nine years to be adjudicated for deportation.

Last year, an immigration judge released him on $1,500 bond. His case, along with that of other immigrants who've been held in detention for long periods, is before the U.S. Supreme Court. Oral arguments were heard Nov. 30. At issue is whether it violates the Constitution to subject immigrants facing criminal deportation to long-term detention without bond hearings.

For now, Owino works at a farmers market in San Diego, selling Kenyan food as he waits to hear his fate. He is worried about what will happen to him if he's deported to Kenya. The police there, he said, have long memories. "They will kill me for sure."

Organizations to Contact

The editors have compiled the following list of organizations concerned with the issues debated in this book. The descriptions are derived from materials provided by the organizations. All have publications or information available for interested readers. This list was compiled on the date of publication of the present volume; the information provided here may change. Be aware that many organizations take several weeks or longer to respond to inquiries, so allow as much time as possible.

American Immigration Council
1331 G Street NW
Suite 200
Washington, DC 20005
phone: (202) 507-7500
email: wfeliz@immcouncil.org
website: http://www.americanimmigrationcouncil.org

The American Immigration Council promotes laws, policies, and attitudes that honor the United States' proud history as a nation of immigrants.

Black Alliance for Just Immigration
phone: (347) 410-5312
website: http://blackalliance.org

The Black Alliance for Just Immigration (BAJI) believes that African Americans and black immigrants are stronger together and can be leaders in the fight against structural racism and systemic discrimination.

Families for Freedom
35 West 31st Street, #702
New York, NY 10001
phone: (646) 290-8720
website: http://familiesforfreedom.org

Families for Freedom is run by and for families facing and fighting deportation. Its membership includes immigrant prisoners (detainees), former immigrant prisoners, their loved ones, and individuals at risk of deportation.

The Hebrew Immigrant Aid Society (HIAS)
1300 Spring Street, Suite 500
Silver Spring, MD 20910
phone: (301) 844-7300
website: http://www.hias.org

HIAS's mission is to rescue people whose lives are in danger for being who they are. It protects the most vulnerable refugees, helping them build new lives and reuniting them with their families in safety and freedom.

Immigrant Defense Project
40 West 39th Street, Fifth Floor
New York, NY 10018
phone: (212) 725-6422
website: http://www.immigrantdefenseproject.org

The Immigrant Defense Project works to transform a racially biased criminal legal system that violates basic human rights and an immigration system that tears hundreds of thousands of immigrants with convictions from their homes and families.

Immigrant Legal Resource Center (ILRC)
1663 Mission Street, Suite 602
San Francisco, CA 94103
phone: (415) 255-9499
email: hleung@ilrc.org
website: http://www.ilrc.org

ILRC works with immigrants, community organizations, and the legal sector to continue to build a democratic society that values diversity and the rights of all people.

Immigrant Youth Justice League (IYJL)
4753 North Broadway
Suite 904
Chicago, IL 60640
email: info@iyjl.org
website: http://www.iyjl.org

IYJL is led by undocumented organizers working toward full recognition of the rights and contributions of all immigrants through education, leadership development, policy advocacy, resource gathering, and mobilization.

Immigration Voice
1177 Branham Lane, #321
San Jose, CA 95118
phone: (202) 386-6250
email: info@immigrationvoice.org
website: http://immigrationvoice.org

Immigration Voice organizes grassroots efforts to solve several problems in the employment-based green card process, including delays due to retrogression, delays due to USCIS processing backlogs, and delays due to labor certification backlogs.

Migration Policy Institute
1400 16th Street NW, Suite 300
Washington, DC 20036
phone: (202) 266-1940
email: info@migrationpolicy.org
website: http://www.migrationpolicy.org

The Migration Policy Institute is an independent, nonpartisan, nonprofit think tank in Washington, DC, dedicated to analysis of the movement of people worldwide.

National Immigration Law Center
3450 Wilshire Boulevard, #108–62
Los Angeles, CA 90010
phone: (213) 639-3900
email: reply@nilc.org
website: http://www.nilc.org

Established in 1979, the National Immigration Law Center (NILC) is one of the leading organizations in the United States exclusively dedicated to defending and advancing the rights of immigrants with low income.

United We Dream
email: info@unitedwedream.org
website: http://unitedwedream.org

United We Dream is the largest immigrant youth-led organization in the nation. It organizes and advocates for the dignity and fair treatment of immigrant youth and families, regardless of immigration status.

Welcoming America
PO Box 2554
Decatur, GA 30031
phone: (404) 631-6593
website: http://www.welcomingamerica.org

A nonprofit, nonpartisan organization, Welcoming America is proud to support the many diverse communities and partners who are leading efforts to make their communities more vibrant places for all.

Bibliography

Books

Amada Armenta. *Protect, Serve, and Deport: The Rise of Policing as Immigration Enforcement.* Oakland, CA: University of California Press, 2017.

Aviva Chomski. *Undocumented: How Immigration Became Illegal.* Boston, MA: Beacon Press, 2014.

David A. Gerber. *American Immigration: A Very Short Introduction.* New York, NY: Oxford University Press, 2011.

Tanya Maria Golash-Boza. *Deported: Immigrant Policing, Disposable Labor and Global Capitalism.* New York, NY: NYU Press, 2015.

Torrie Hester. *Deportation: The Origin of U.S. Policy.* Philadelphia, PA: University of Pennsylvania Press, 2017.

Daniel Kanstroom. *Deportation Nation: Outsiders in American History.* Cambridge, MA: Harvard University Press, 2010.

Nisha Kapoor. *Deport, Deprive, Extradite: 21st Century State Extremism.* New York, NY: Penguin Random House, 2018.

Ekaterina Mouratova. *The Complete Guide to U.S. Immigration Law.* New York, NY: Law Firm of Ekaterina Mouratova, 2017.

William Perez. *We Are Americans: Undocumented Students Pursuing the American Dream.* Sterling, VA: Stylus, 2009.

Tisha M. Rajendra. *Migrants and Citizens: Justice and Responsibility in the Ethics of Immigration.* Grand Rapids, MI: William B. Eerdmans, 2017.

Robyn Magalit Rodriguez. *In Lady Liberty's Shadow: The Politics of Race and Immigration in New Jersey.* New Brunswick, NJ: Rutgers University Press, 2017.

Sara Saedi. *Americanized: Rebel Without a Green Card*. New York, NY: Knopf, 2018.

Paola Tinoco. *U.S. Immigration Made Easy: Understanding Immigration Law*. Phoenix, AZ: Jones Media Publishing, 2017.

Leon Wildes. *John Lennon vs. The U.S.A.: The Inside Story of the Most Bitterly Contested and Influential Deportation Case in United States History*. New York, NY: Ankerwycke, 2016.

Kent Wong. *Dreams Deported: Immigrant Youth and Families Resist Deportation*. Los Angeles, CA: UCLA Press, 2013.

Luis Zayas. *Forgotten Citizens: Deportation, Children, and the Making of American Exiles and Orphans*. New York, NY: Oxford University Press, 2015.

Periodicals and Internet Sources

Kate Aronoff, "Climate Change and the Deportation Machine: A Match Forged in Hell, Hurricane Harvey Edition," In These Times, August 25, 2017. http://inthesetimes .com/article/20461/hurricane-harvey-climate-change -deportation-immigration-incarceration-Texas.

Michael Arria, "Why Defending Workers' Rights Means Fighting ICE's Deportation Machine," Salon, August 26, 2017. http://www.salon.com/2017/08/27/why-defending -workers-rights-means-fighting-ices-deportation-machine_ partner.

Alvaro M. Bedova, "Deportation Is Going High-Tech Under Trump," *Atlantic*, June 21, 2017. https://www .theatlantic.com/technology/archive/2017/06/data-driven -deportation/531090.

Brian Bennett, "Not Just 'Bad Hombres': Trump Is Targeting Up to 8 Million People for Deportation," *Los Angeles Times*, February 4, 2017. http://www.latimes.com/politics/ la-na-pol-trump-deportations-20170204-story.html.

Kenya Downs, Irish Immigrant's Arrest Highlights Race's Role in Deportation, BBC News, July 23, 2017. http://www.bbc.com/news/world-us-canada-40332646.

Ginger Adams Otis, "Family Devastated After Long Island Father Detained for Deportation," *New York Daily News*, August 26, 2017. http://www.nydailynews.com/new-york/family-devastated-father-detained-deportation-article-1.3443754.

Peter Rothberg and Rosy Alvarez, "Andres Magana Ortiz's Deportation Is Indefensible. Help Reverse It," *Nation*, August 11, 2017. https://www.thenation.com/article/andres-magana-ortizs-deportation-is-indefensible-help-reverse-it.

Sarah Stillman, "The Mothers Being Deported by Trump," *New Yorker*, July 22, 2017. http://www.newyorker.com/news/news-desk/the-mothers-being-deported-by-trump.

Esther Yu Hsi Lee, "ICE Detains Immigrant Mom Protected from Deportation," ThinkProgress, August 24, 2017. https://thinkprogress.org/daca-recipients-deportation-4273dbfee10f.

Index